for Jenna and Philip Mead

THE WINTER'S TALE

John Lucas

GREENWICH EXCHANGE
LONDON

Greenwich Exchange, London

First published in Great Britain in 2005
All rights reserved

Shakespeare's The Winter's Tale © John Lucas 2005

Printed and bound by Q3 Digital/Litho, Loughborough
Tel: 01509 213456
Typesetting and layout by Albion Associates, London
Tel: 020 8852 4646
Cover design by December Publications, Belfast
Tel: 028 90286559

Cover picture: Mary Evans Picture Library

Greenwich Exchange Website: www.greenex.co.uk
ISBN 1-87155-80-3

Contents

Introduction

In 1588 Robert Greene, dramatist and professional writer, published *Pandosto. The Triumph of Time. Wherein is discovered by a pleasant History, that although by the means of sinister fortune Truth may be concealed, yet by Time, in spite of fortune, it is most manifestly revealed.* A little more than 20 years later Shakespeare transformed Greene's tedious prose romance into one of the greatest plays in the canon. He did so, most commentators agree, without much changing Greene's story or introducing or excluding many characters of the original. But the changes are of the utmost importance. Thereby, we might say, hangs the Tale. For example, in Greene it is the wronged queen, Bellaria, who asks that the Oracle be consulted, and at the end of her trial she dies. As for the King of Bohemia, Pandosto, he commits suicide when at last he realises he has falsely accused his wife of adultery. In Shakespeare's play, Leontes, who has disbelieved the report from the Oracle he himself has sought, lives on to repent the death, as he thinks, of Hermione. Greene's Capnio becomes in Autolycus a far more interesting character. But most crucial of all, Greene has no equivalent for Paulina. She is Shakespeare's invention. She is, moreover, the one character in the play with a Christian name, and the significance of this will be discussed later. Here I want to ask the question, what kind of a play is *The Winter's Tale*?

Samuel Johnson, whose *Preface to Shakespeare* I would advise anyone coming fresh to the plays to read ahead of any other commentary, wonderfully remarked that Shakespeare's plays are not:

> in the rigorous and critical sense either tragedies or comedies, but compositions of a distinct kind; exhibiting the real state of sublunary nature, which partakes of good and evil, joy and sorrow, mingled with endless variety of proportion and innumerable modes of combination; and expressing the course of the world, in which the loss of one is the gain of another; in which, at the same time, the reveller is hasting to his wine,

and the mourner burying his friend; in which the malignity of
one is sometimes defeated by the frolick of another; and many
mischiefs and many benefits are done and hindered without
design.

With this in mind, consider The Shepherd's "Thou met'est with
things dying, I with things new-born." The "rigorous and critical
sense" Johnson refers to is that according to which tragedy and
comedy are altogether different kinds, distinguished not merely by
actorly convention (the buskin – a kind of thick-soled boot worn by
actors of tragedies in the ancient Athenian theatre and the sock, its
comic equivalent), but by different 'rules' which date back to Aristotle
and were developed by Roman dramatists. To be sure, Elizabethan
dramatists called their plays Comedies and Tragedies, but
Shakespeare, as Johnson realises, is not to be judged by the rules of
others. If, then, we call *The Winter's Tale* a tragi-comedy, as is
commonly done, we need to remember that while a mixture of farce
and Machiavellian savagery was becoming increasingly popular in
the Jacobean theatre, Shakespeare's play cannot usefully be compared
to such examples as Cyril Tourneur's *Revenger's Tragedy* (1607) or
The White Devil (1612) by John Webster. For one thing, though his
play contains deaths, of young as well as old (Mamillius and
Antigonus) it does not end tragically. For another, it draws on material
that deliberately eschews the kind of realism Tourneur and Webster
work with. In *The Winter's Tale* a good man becomes more or less
inexplicably mad with sexual jealousy, another is chased and eaten
by a bear, that which was lost is found, a statue comes to life. To
repeat, what kind of play is this?

In his poem, 'Autolycus', Louis MacNeice says of Shakespeare
in his late period:

> Eclectic always, now extravagant,
> Sighting his matter through a timeless prism
> He ranged his classical bric-à-brac in grottos
> Where knights of Ancient Greece had Latin mottoes
> And fishermen their flapjacks – none should want
> Colour for lack of an anachronism.

MacNeice here wittily fingers Shakespeare's supreme indifference
to what we might call surface realism in his late plays. That Bohemia

had no sea-coast, that Julio (or Giulio) Romano (c1492-1546) was an artist of the Italian Renaissance and so could hardly have been known to earlier ages, that no woman in pre-Christian Sicilia, or elsewhere for that matter, could have been called Paulina, these are obvious affronts to historical accuracy. (Although as far as I know, the huge importance of the last anachronism has not been discussed.) Equally obvious are the links between *The Winter's Tale* and the other late plays, *Pericles*, *Cymbeline*, and *The Tempest*, all four of them written some time between 1609-11. All have something to say about the matter of Nature versus Nurture, all make use of fairytale or romance elements, and three feature lost or cast-away daughters who in different ways become through the agency of time found and thereby reconciled to their tempestuous fathers. Little of this is entirely new: you have only to think of the bastard Falconbridge in *King John*, of *A Midsummer Night's Dream*, of the relationship between Lear and Cordelia, to realise that familiar material is being re-worked. What matters is the way it is re-worked. Moreover, the concern with Time has in *The Winter's Tale* an added dimension, as has the debate over Nature versus Nurture.

There is also the poetry. I don't see it is possible to experience these late plays without recognising that they are connected not merely by theme but by a style that feels qualitatively different from anything that has gone before. In his little-regarded study, *Shakespeare* (1936), John Middleton Murry put his finger on the crucial point when he compared speeches from all four plays. First, Marina in *Pericles*:

> No, I will rob Tellus of her weed
> To strew thy green with flowers; the yellows, blues,
> The purple violets, and marigolds,
> Shall as a carpet hang upon thy grave,
> While summer days do last.
>
> (Act IV, scene 1, 14-18)

Next, Arvigerus in *Cymbeline*:

> With fairest flowers
> Whilst summer lasts, and I live here, Fidele,
> I'll sweeten thy sad grave, thou shalt not lack
> The flower that's like thy face, pale primrose, nor

The azured harebell, like thy veins, no, nor
The leaf of eglantine, whom not to slander,
Outsweeten'd not thy breath.

(Act IV, scene 2, 218-224)

Then, Perdita:

Now my fairs't friend,
I would I had some flowers o' th' spring, that might
Become your time of day – and yours, and yours,
That wear upon your virgin branches yet
Your maidenheads growing. O Proserpina,
For the flowers now that, frighted, thou let'st fall
From Dis's wagon! Daffodils,
That come before the swallow dares, and take
The winds of March with beauty; violets, dim,
But sweeter than the lids of Juno's eyes
Or Cytherea's breath; pale primroses
That die unmarried ere they can behold
Bright Phoebus in his strength ...

(Act IV, scene 4, 112-124)

And finally, the song of Iris to Ceres in the masque scene in *The Tempest*, commending her:

... banks with pioned and twilled brims,
Which spongy April at thy hest betrims,
To make cold nymphs chaste crowns ...

(Act IV, scene 1, 64-6)

The strewing of graves with flowers mingles death and life, acknowledges endings and promises new beginnings, conjoins what dies and what's new-born. And it is surely remarkable, even though Middleton Murry does not remark on the matter, that each of these moments occurs in Act IV of their respective plays. Those fascinated by numerology may make of this what they will. I wish merely to note that in all the plays, the fourth act, as you would expect, begins the move towards new life after the terrible storms of the earlier acts. And I will add that it is in Act IV, scene 7 of *King Lear* that Lear, in "fresh garments", is reconciled to Cordelia, though at first he tells her "You do me wrong to take me out o' the grave". But *King*

Lear, that most terrible of tragedies, ends with the trampling down of any hope for the new or for the rebirth of hope. Herein lies its essential difference from the late plays, which are impregnated with language that accommodates and celebrates such hope.

I became alert to the special quality of the language of *The Winter's Tale* when I co-directed a workshop production of the play in the early 1980s. There are those who have argued and who continue to argue that Shakespeare is best studied on the page, and that the theatre is somehow a distraction to an understanding of his work. I absolutely disagree. It is, I will admit, almost impossible to go through life without seeing bad productions of Shakespeare, but even mediocre ones will necessarily illuminate areas on which the lamp of the study cannot hope to throw light. Working on *The Winter's Tale* made me realise, among so much else, how important touch is, how the clasping of hands, written into the text, makes us *see* relationships in a manner that we cannot, I am convinced, adequately gauge from the printed page alone. Even having to resolve apparently such simple matters as where X and Y are standing when Z speaks, forces us to consider each scene with a degree of attention that reveals how complete a dramatist Shakespeare is. Well, of course, common sense insists. He was himself an actor, he worked with a regular troupe of players, the King's Men, whose individual quirks and talents he had to cater for, and he was always mindful of the need to entertain his audiences. All true, yet how often and quickly forgotten by commentators who write as though the plays, *The Winter's Tale* no less and no more than the others, are remote from what Yeats called "theatre business". In what follows I hope to consider the play at all times as a work of art that comes fully alive only when it is performed, or at all events when it is thought of as taking place on stage.

A Note on the Text

There is no Quarto version of *The Winter's Tale*. That is to say, no printed text of the play earlier than the Folio survives. The Folio edition of Shakespeare's works was produced in 1623, seven years after the writer's death, and although its compilers, Heminge and Condell, clearly took great pains to make their texts as accurate as possible, we cannot be sure that the text of *The Winter's Tale* is one hundred per cent correct, especially as we have no Quarto versions to compare it with. Quarto refers to size of paper but also to editions of the play published during Shakespeare's lifetime, often from actors' copies or those of stage-managers, or prompters. Such editions were liable to be heavily marked with stage directions. The Folio edition of *The Winter's Tale* has relatively few such directions. (Later editors have added stage directions based on what is happening on stage.) In the following discussion of the play, all stage directions given in italics are taken from the Folio edition, although for the written text itself I have used Ernest Schanzer's Penguin edition, which is based on that which J.H.P. Pafford made for the Arden Shakespeare (1955 and then 1963). It is worth noting that Pafford suggests that the copy of *The Winter's Tale* on which the Folio printer draws was transcribed by Ralph Crane, a professional scribe, and is "an exceptionally good text, with few signs of corruption."

1

Hospitality and Jealousy

The Winter's Tale opens with two courtiers exchanging formal politenesses about the visit, now coming to its end, of Polixenes, King of Bohemia, to his old friend, Leontes, King of Sicilia. Archidamus speaks for Bohemia, apologising to Camillo, a Sicilian Lord, for the poor "entertainment" that will be on offer when the Sicilian court pays a return visit. He means to compliment his hosts on the splendour of their entertainment. The men have plainly just come from a feast and Archidamus is, not to put too fine a point on it, rather the worse for wear. He stumbles over his words: "we cannot with such magnificence, in so rare – I know not what to say. We will give you sleepy drinks, that your senses, unintelligent of our insufficience, may, though they cannot praise us, as little accuse us." Such orundity implies someone far gone in drink: "I know not what to say". But what he does say is sufficient in its woozy manner (how he wraps his tongue round "unintelligent of our insufficience") to prompt Camillo's wry rejoinder: "You pay a great deal too dear for what's given freely."

The phrase "given freely" is, however, when linked with "entertainment", about to set up reverberations that will echo throughout the play. For entertainment, we need to note, means both 'to treat at table' and 'to receive hospitality' and this, as we shall see, is of crucial importance to a play in which hospitality is both of the essence and appallingly perverted. But now Archidamus adds "you shall see, as I have said, great difference betwixt our Bohemia and your Sicilia." The reference is to differences between the two lands, but it can also hint at differences between the two kings who are the embodiments of their respective countries.

And, indeed, for all that Camillo's major speech now insists on the close and enduring friendship between Leontes and Polixenes, it also points to an inevitable distance between them. The kings "were trained together in their childhoods," he says, "and there rooted betwixt them then such an affection, which cannot choose but branch now." Still intimately connected, yet growing apart. And as though to strengthen his contention, he adds (in a moment of the speech easily overlooked) that since their boyhood they have never again met: "their encounters, though not personal, hath been royally attorneyed with interchange of gifts, letters, loving embassies: that they have seemed to be together, though absent; shook hands as over a vast; and embraced, as it were, from the ends of opposed winds. The heavens continue their loves!"

"I think there is not in the world either malice or matter to alter it", Archidamus at once replies. And he then goes on to extol the virtues of Leontes' young son, Mamillius, praise which Camillo is happy to endorse and even embellish – Mamillius, he assures the other man, "physics the subject, makes old hearts fresh." Like a restorative medicine, the prince guarantees the continued health of Sicilia.

It is all both suavely done and reassuring. Though they have not actually shaken hands or embraced since boyhood, the two kings are, we are given to understand, clasped in enduring friendship. And yet there are ripples on the surface of this content. Why else should Camillo immediately follow his claim that the kings have "embraced, as it were, from the ends of opposed winds", by adding, "The heavens continue their loves!" When Heminge and Condell brought out the first collected edition of Shakespeare's works in 1623, they did not include the exclamation mark at the end of Camillo's speech. That virtually all modern editors print this added emphasis is, therefore, an interpretation of Camillo's meaning, but one that is surely justified. For Archidamus' reply, while containing a proleptic irony he can hardly be expected to understand, betrays a possible uneasiness, as though in seeking to reassure Camillo he wants also to reassure himself. We can imagine the two men exchanging glances which say more than their mere words. And so his hurrying on to tell Camillo that "You have an unspeakable comfort of your young prince Mamillius" can be a way of saying that whatever doubts there may be about the present, the future is assured.

At which point the royal parties sweep onstage, Polixenes and his 'brother' in conversation as they come. He must go home, he says, having already stayed for nine months, and he is worried at what may be happening in Bohemia during his absence. A reasonable fear, and one that Polixenes repeats in order to extricate himself from Leontes' pressing request that he stay longer. Leontes then turns to Hermione. Perhaps she can succeed where he has failed.

And so for the first time Hermione speaks, stepping forward as she does so, we have surely to imagine, to join the men. But notice that although she may glance across at Polixenes, she addresses her words to Leontes. Until the moment, that is, when she turns to Polixenes himself and says, playfully:

> Yet of your royal presence I'll adventure
> The borrow of a week. When at Bohemia
> You take my lord, I'll give him my commission
> To let him there a month behind the gest
> Prefix'd for's parting;

Then back to her husband:

> ... yet, good deed, Leontes,
> I love thee not a jar o' th'clock behind
> What lady she her lord.

Then, again to Polixenes, "You'll stay?"

But he won't. And so she tries once more, this time more determinedly, as though her powers of persuasion are being put to the test. "You shall not go," she tells him, "Will you go yet?/Force me to keep you as a prisoner,/Not like a guest." It seems reasonable to suppose that when she says this she matches her action to her words by laying a hand on his arm, taking him prisoner, as it were. And it does the trick. Polixenes gives in. "Your guest, then, madam." To which she replies that she is pleased to be "Not your gaoler, then,/ But your kind hostess."

Hermione is indeed the embodiment of hospitality. "Kind" in Shakespeare's day, as in our own, meant not only generous, but 'having the nature of'. And it is as kind hostess that she now begins to question him about the boyhood he shared with her husband. She lets him do the talking, only interrupting him when he pays her the perhaps ambiguous compliment of telling her that he and Leontes were closest "in those unfledged days [when] was my wife a girl;/ Your precious self had then not crossed the eyes/Of my young playfellow." Playfully, Hermione says:

> Th' offences we have made you do we'll answer,
> If you first sinned with us, and that with us
> You did continue fault, and that you slipped not
> With any but with us.

Leontes: Is he won yet?

Hermione: He'll stay, my lord.

Leontes: At my request he would not.
> Hermione, my dearest, thou never spok'st
> To better purpose.

This prompts the obvious question, where has Leontes been while Hermione has stood listening to Polixenes? For it is evident that only towards the end of her words does he again come within earshot. "Is he won yet?" What has he heard? It is at least conceivable that he overhears her say "If you first sinned with us" and misunderstood "us" not as a reference to the two girls who had captured the young men's hearts but as the royal 'We', and thus referring to Hermione alone. And if this is so, then we have some explanation for his jealousy, even if this scarcely amounts to justification.

Hermione, it scarcely needs saying, can have no sense of how her words may have been misinterpreted. Besides, she is doing Leontes' bidding in persuading Polixenes to stay, and so, delighting in her success, she rallies her husband:

> What? Have I twice said well? When was't before?
> I prithee tell me. Cram's with praise, and make's
> As fat as tame things.

The untroubled colloquialisms, "was't", "cram's", "make's", the lovely wit of "as fat as tame things" (from a heavily pregnant woman), the almost drowsed movement of the lines, bespeak a contented fullness. But this is lost on Leontes, or misunderstood by him. For now, as though putting her to the test, he reminds her that it was three months before "I could make thee open thy white hand/And clap thyself my love: then didst thou utter/'I am yours for ever'."

Again, action must suit the words. He will open her hand, place his over it, and repeat her pledge of undying loyalty "I am yours for ever", in which it is of the utmost importance that he should use the plural form of the second person: "yours", not "thine", though he refers to her as "thou". Hermione, in other words, is his subject. This distinction between plural and singular is an anglicised version of the French 'vous'/'tu', still retained, though not consistently, from the days when the official court language in England was French. 'Vous' is formal, polite, as well as the plural 'you'/'tu', as well as the singular is informal, familiar. Social inferiors may be addressed as 'thee', social superiors must always be 'you'. It is a distinction made much of in the history plays, and it counts here, too, in Leontes' mode of speaking to Hermione, in which familiarity can blend, not necessarily easily, with his claim to have a standing over hers. He is not merely husband and lover, he is king, and on both counts Hermione must heed her subservient role. So, at least, that use of the plural pronoun will surely imply.

But as well a loyal wife Hermione is also a kind hostess. And so, wittily, deftly, she acknowledges her twin identity, double responsibilities. "Why, lo you now," she tells Leontes, "I have spoke to th'purpose twice:/The one for ever earned a royal husband;" and we can imagine her repeating his word "ever" with due emphasis before she turns to Polixenes and says: "Th'other for some while a friend." After which a stage direction reads [*giving her hand to Pol.*] The direction is not in the Folio but it is what Hermione does, plain enough. Hence Leontes' twisted view of them "paddling palms and pinching fingers ... O, that is entertainment/My bosom likes not." Remembering Archidamus' use of the word "entertainment" we can now see how Leontes is turning it to corrupt ends.

*   *   *

Can there be any justification for Leontes' perverted account? Only, I think, if we assume that he chooses to read Hermione's demonstration of hospitality, of amity, as personal, private, and therefore suspect. Here, then, we need to step back and consider the appearance of the word "amity", late on in *The Winter's Tale*. When Florizel and Perdita escape Polixenes' rage by fleeing to Sicilia, they are met by the chastened Leontes, who tells Florizel that:

> ... I lost –
> All my own folly – the society,
> Amity too, of your brave father ...
>
> (Act V, scene 1, 133-135)

The same word crops up at an important point in *The Merchant of Venice* where Lorenzo tells Portia, "Madam, although I speak it in your presence,/You have a noble and a true conceit/Of god-like amity". (Act III, scene 4). At this moment Bassanio has had to go to the assistance of his friend, Antonio, who is threatened with ruin by the loss of his ships. Lorenzo praises Portia because, he says, she understands the twin claims on Bassanio: of love for her and friendship for Antonio.

In *The Winter's Tale* Hermione seeks to reconcile her love for Leontes with his friendship with Polixenes. And amity is most fittingly expressed in the taking of hands. Indeed, in Renaissance emblem literature 'concord', which means amity, is always imaged by a pair of clasped hands. Hospitality, concord, amity – they intertwine, are variations on each other. But you have only to think how the formal act of dancers holding each other can pass over into a more intimate embrace, or be perceived so to do, to understand that Leontes may imagine himself justified in his (mis)reading of how Hermione clasps the hand of a friend he hasn't seen since boyhood. And from this, the terrible inversion of love and friendship follow.

For as the long scene unfolds, so Leontes' sexual imaginings become wilder, and, especially disturbing, it seems to me, are *indulged*, as though a force within him is licensing his imagination. When he tells his son to "Go play, boy, play" the word prompts him to add "thy mother plays, and I /Play too – but so disgraced a part." Throughout his career Shakespeare will pun on "acting": we are rarely allowed to forget that what we are watching is a show. But here Leontes becomes so caught up in his act that it takes control of him. He raves that many a man has been cuckolded by his wife: "That little thinks she has been sluiced in's absence,/And his pond fished by his next neighbour ..." Leontes' hysterical rage is focused on the word "sluiced", its disgust compounded by the fact that as the line is uttered all emphasis inevitably falls on it.

He has now to convince others that, as he tells Camillo, "My wife is slippery." And when Camillo dares to doubt Leontes, the king answers him in a speech which shows how far he has allowed his imagination to twist what he and we have seen of Hermione's hospitable entertainment of Polixenes:

> Is whispering nothing?
> Is leaning cheek to cheek? Is meeting noses?
> Kissing with inside lip? Stopping the career
> Of laughter with a sigh – a note infallible
> Of breaking honesty. Horsing foot on foot?
> Skulking in corners? Wishing clocks more swift?
> Hours, minutes? Noon midnight? And all eyes
> Blind with the pin and web but theirs, theirs only ...

[Note: "pin and web", the disease of cataract]

Try speaking these lines aloud and you become caught up in their hysterical exultance, the increased hammering emphases. Note in particular how as you come round the line ending of "and all eyes", your voice will hit the word "Blind" with especial force. Leontes is telling Camillo that the courtier cannot afford to trust the evidence of his own eyes. You are blind, like the rest of them, he means. I alone can see what's going on.

But Camillo, to his credit, resists Leontes' ravings:

> Good my lord, be cured
> Of this diseased opinion, and betimes,
> For 'tis most dangerous.

It takes some nerve to tell an absolute ruler that he's mad, and Camillo's courage and integrity are not to be underestimated. I suspect Shakespeare's first audiences would have stirred uncomfortably when Leontes goes on to order Camillo to poison Polixenes, and that "To do this deed,/Promotion follows." There were rumours aplenty of James' court as a place where enemies of the king, real or supposed, could well end up dead and poison, it was suggested, had put an end to more than one of them. In Act II, scene 1, Leontes will in fact declare, "There is a plot against my life, my crown," by which time he probably believes it.

But for now, thinking he has persuaded Camillo to do his bidding, he exits, leaving Camillo to explain to Polixenes, who has returned, that his life is in danger. Best get away, Camillo tells him, and:

> ... For myself, I'll put
> My fortunes to your service, which are here
> By this discovery lost. Be not uncertain,
> For, by the honour of my parents, I
> Have uttered truth ...

Polixenes: I do believe thee:
I saw his heart in's face. Give me thy hand ...

"Be not uncertain". We can imagine Polixenes wondering whether Camillo's offer to go with him is a trick, a way of hustling him off the premises precisely to do Leontes' bidding. But with "Give me thy hand" Polixenes decides to trust Camillo, and their handshake symbolises the accord, indeed concord, between them, even though social decorum is preserved. Camillo addresses Polixenes by the plural form of pronoun – "Your service" – whereas Polixenes says to Camillo, "I do believe thee." This may seem unimportant, but will have profound implications when Polixenes comes face to face with the seeming shepherdess his son loves. Decorum can also mean recognition of distinction, of distance between king and commoner. Whether such distinction is a matter of Nurture or Nature is of course central to the play's meaning.

*   *   *

Before we leave Act I, scene 2, I need briefly to consider how best to account for Leontes' mad, sexual jealousy. It is clearly unlike Othello's. As Matt Simpson says in his monograph on that play, "the declarations both the Moor and Desdemona make are perhaps best seen as expressions of faith and good intention rather than the statements of people who understand what their sudden marriage is based on and requires. Let's not forget that their marriage is an elopement ..." Othello and Desdemona are new to each other, and each, as far as the other is concerned, is literally exotic. This makes it easier for Iago to pour the poison of doubt into Othello's mind. But Lcontes and Hermione are years into a marriage that already has produced a son and that seems to be as much founded on trust as on loving companionship. (The one is surely inconceivable without the other?) We can speculate, if we wish, that until the moment of Polixenes' arrival at court, Hermione will have met few if any men of worth, though this seems pointless. Besides, nobody sets out to convince Leontes that his wife is being unfaithful. Nobody, that is, but himself. What he interprets as signs of infidelity are no more than evidence that Hermione is doing as he wishes and as she chooses: revealing herself to be the embodiment of hospitality. If then, we label Leontes' fixation 'paranoia', as some have done, and bearing in mind that the term means "mental illness characterised by delusions of persecutions, of sexual jealousy, or exaggerated self-importance", we will be substituting a psychological explanation for the meta-physical term 'evil', which earlier critics more usually accepted, and which took little note of how Hermione's acting out her part, innocent though it is, could contribute to Leontes' terrible delusions.

I am not sure that a full explanation of what happens to Leontes is to be sought, much less supplied, though as watchers of what happens on stage we can see what he sees and can therefore understand why he might, just might, react as he does. And if this seems evasive, let me quote two remarks from Samuel Johnson's *History of Rasselas: Prince of Abyssinia* (1759), that omnium gatherum of stoic wisdom: "Misfortunes ... should always be expected ... the angels of affliction spread their toils alike for the virtuous and the wicked, for the mighty and the mean." (ch. 38). And "to mock the heaviest of human affliction [madness] is neither charitable nor wise ... Of the uncertainties of our present state, the most ... dreadful and alarming is the uncertain continuance of reason." (ch. 43). The great Scottish enlightenment philosopher, David Hume, argued that a full explanation of causation required what he called the presence of both sufficient and necessary causes. We demand plausibility for what characters say and do. We require satisfactory explanations. We want an answer to the question 'why'.

Sometimes those explanations are external (a bolt of lightning, an unlooked-for accident), but for the most part they are to be sought in the nature of the character. Character is action, action is character, in Henry James' words. But however hard we strive for an understanding of, or explanation for Leontes' slide into the madness that seizes him, something in it remains opaque, lost in the deep, dark recesses of the human heart. Yes, he may overhear Hermione tell Polixenes that "you first sinned with us," but then common sense would tell him she can't be referring to adulterous behaviour. (She makes no attempt to whisper the words.) Yes, he may then discover his imagination seizing hold of him so that his words become feverish speculation that feeds the appetite; he may even – who knows? – unconsciously want to assert authority as king of Sicilia and then discover that this is dragging him out of kilter. But none of these possible explanations can, either singly or put together, amount to sufficient and necessary reasons for his ravings. Johnson's sombre words about the "heaviest of human affliction", the sad forbearance of his remark that to "mock" this is "neither charitable nor wise", must therefore give us pause. That Leontes is afflicted we can all agree. What matters now is less the cause of that affliction than its consequences, for himself and others.

*   *   *

It is therefore apposite that at the beginning of Act II, scene 1, Mamillius, wishing to humour his mother, who as yet knows nothing of Leontes' mad suspicions, should offer to tell her a story: "A sad tale's best for winter. I have one/Of sprites and goblins." Evil or harmful spirits, he means. At which point, enter Leontes. Mamillius is taken away from her and Leontes confronts Hermione with the claim that she is both adulteress and traitor, and that Camillo, whose escape is now known, is "A fedary with her." He orders her to be taken to prison.

Hermione's response is one of utter bewilderment and, then, resignation:

> There's some ill planet reigns.
> I must be patient till the heavens look
> With an aspect more favourable.

Hermione, that is, doesn't put the blame on Leontes for what has happened. Her belief that "the heavens" will make all come well introduces a note of which more will be said later, although at this stage of the play we have no reason to assume that her words amount to more than conventional piety. There is, however, far more than convention at issue in her departing words:

> Do not weep, good fools:
> There is no cause. When you shall know your mistress
> Has deserved prison, then abound in tears
> As I come out. This action I now go on
> Is for my better grace. Adieu, my lord.
> I never wished to see you sorry: now
> I trust I shall.

The opening words are spoken to her women. Their mixture of calm resolution and inner certainty bear remarkable testimony to her integrity. They speak for her more eloquently than any protestation of innocence could. And her trust in the "heavens" takes on a specific Christian note when she speaks of "better grace". In the Arden edition, Pafford remarks that as "Hermione has no doubt of her own purity", this can hardly be intended to suggest that her soul is being refined through purgatory. But this is unduly literalistic. The postlapsarian soul is incapable of avoiding impurity, no matter how blameless a life its possessor lives. What matters is Hermione's recognition of imperfection – a recognition that places her at odds with her husband, who can see no wrong in his own behaviour. Hence, her words to him, which are uttered not in a spirit of anger or desire for retribution but come from a concern for his welfare. *For his own sake* he needs to understand the truth. Magnanimity can hardly go further.

But though she will not plead her innocence, Hermione does not lack for others to do it for her, among them Antigonus, as brave as Camillo in daring to oppose the king's delusions. "You are abused," he tells Leontes, "and by some putter-on/That will be damned for't./Would I knew the villain!/I would lam-damn him." No commentator has come up with a satisfactory explanation for the phrase "lam-damn", but it goes with Antigonus' attempt to make sense of an accusation that has left him and the other Lords accompanying Leontes aghast. He is made still more aghast by Leontes' brutal loss of civility. The King tells him:

> You smell this business with a sense as cold
> As is a dead man's nose; but I do see't and feel't
> As you feel doing thus …

"Thus" indicates that at this point Leontes tweaks Antigonus' nose, a violently uncivil gesture that is the polar opposite of amity or concord. But deranged though Leontes most certainly is, Antigonus continues to stand up to him, and so in his turn Leontes tells him that to prove his case he has "dispatched in post/To sacred Delphos, to Apollo's temple,/Cleomenes and Dion." This is an important change from *Pandosto*, where it was Queen Bellaria who had sent to Delphos in an attempt to clear her name. Pandosto could claim that she had rigged the reply. But Leontes will be unable to do that.

2

Paulina's Role

The next scene opens "Enter Paulina, a Gentleman, and Attendants." Even more than "Exit, pursued by a bear", this seems to me the most notable stage direction in the entire play. For there is no Paulina in Greene's Romance, any more than there is an Antigonus. Why then does Shakespeare invent them? Antigonus' presence can be more readily accounted for. He is one more male voice of authoritative dissent whom Leontes in his madness refuses to credit. To be sure, he is fully fleshed out – one reason actors love playing Shakespeare is that even the most minor characters have a satisfying dimensionality about them – and in his comparatively few speeches we discover that Antigonus is the father of three daughters, is admirably plain-spoken if limited in intellect (hence his jumping to the "common sense" conclusion that someone must have been whispering lies in Leontes' ear), is courageous and capable of real tenderness. Like his wife he stands up to Leontes.

But Paulina is a far more extraordinary character. When we first meet her she has come to the prison to see Hermione. The gaoler, who tells her he knows her "For a worthy lady,/And one who much I honour", nevertheless daren't risk allowing the two women to meet. Paulina is contemptuous: "Here's ado/To lock up honesty and honour from/Th' access of gentle visitors!" She is permitted to see Emilia, one of Hermione's women, who tells her that the queen has given birth to:

> A daughter, and a goodly babe
> Lusty, and like to live. The Queen receives
> Much comfort in 't; says, 'My poor prisoner,
> I am innocent as you'.

Paulina: I dare be sworn.
        These dangerous, unsafe lunes i' th' King, beshrew
              them!
        He must be told on't, and he shall. The office
        Becomes a woman best. I'll take't upon me.
        If I prove honey-mouthed, let my tongue blister,
        And never to my red-looked anger be
        The trumpet any more.

Paulina as termagent. More, Paulina as warrior-like champion of another woman. There have been hints of such a woman in earlier plays. Rosalind in *As You Like It* goes into exile with her cousin, Celia, and though socially inferior is the doughtier of the two, quicker-witted, more able to discompose male assurance. And Beatrice in *Much Ado About Nothing* is even wittier in her jousting with and discomforting of Benedick. She also has one moment of absolute seriousness, when, outraged by Claudio's leaving her cousin, Hero, at the altar – Claudio believes Hero has deceived him – she challenges Benedick, who, employing a cliché often used by lovers, has just said that he will do anything for her, to "kill Claudio". Although this is often played for laughs, and although it is perhaps inevitable that laughter should be a first reaction to what seems so outrageous a demand, Beatrice means what she says. At all events, she wants her cousin to be avenged. And here, it should be noted that the episode in *Much Ado About Nothing* foreshadows what will happen in *The Winter's Tale*. Hearing herself denounced for what Claudio believes to be her sexual looseness, the girl falls into a faint. The Friar who has been summonsed to marry the pair then suggests that he and the others still present should hide Hero and give it out that she has died:

        When he [Claudio] shall hear she died upon his words
        Th'idea of her life shall sweetly creep
        Into his study of imagination,
        And every lovely organ of her life
        Shall come apparell'd in more precious habit,
        More moving, delicate and more full of life,
        Into the eye and prospect of his soul
        Than when she liv'd indeed: then shall he mourn –

If ever love had interest in his liver –
And wish he had not so accused her.
                              (Act IV, scene 1, 223-232)

The trick whereby Claudio had been induced to think he had seen
Hero welcoming another lover is soon cleared up, which, given the
incompetence of the plotters, is hardly surprising. But Beatrice's
powerful declaration of sorority is nevertheless crucial. She is a strong
woman.

So is Paulina. Hence, her decision to confront Leontes with his
newborn daughter. Hence, too, the self-possessed, scornful wit of
her retort to the gaoler, that hapless jobsworth, who worries that he
has no warrant to allow the baby to be taken out of prison:

You need not fear it, sir.
This child was prisoner to the womb, and is
By law and process of great Nature thence
Free and enfranchised; not a party to
The anger of the King …

And with this wonderful, unanswerable rebuke she goes.

And comes into Leontes' presence. The king is "discovered" on
his own, presumably in his nightclothes and in his bedroom (i.e. the
inner space under the musicians' gallery) in mental torment: "No
night nor day no rest!" And now we discover Mamillius, too, is ill.
Leontes explains this to himself as his son's response to Hermione's
"dishonour". Mamillius, he says, "straight declined, drooped, took
it deeply,/Fastened and fixed the shame on't in himself;/Threw off
his spirit, his appetite, his sleep,/And downright languished." It's all
Hermione's fault:

Camillo and Polixenes
Laugh at me, make their pastime at my sorrow.
They should not laugh if I could reach them, nor
Shall she within my power.

At which point Paulina enters, followed by her husband, Antigonus,
lords and servants, all of them trying to prevent her from confronting
Leontes. It is a great visual moment. Paulina, this great force of
nature, will not listen to the voices urging restraint, voices that, as

she says, by their failure to tell Leontes the worst about himself, worsen his condition. (Though to be fair to Camillo and Antigonus, they have tried to reason with him, have refused to believe his accusations of Hermione's adultery.) Nevertheless, Paulina's insistence that she is here to do him good strikes a new note: "I/Do come with words as med'cinal as true,/Honest as either, to purge him of that humour/That presses him from sleep." The intimate connection between sleeplessness and a guilty or troubled conscience is, of course, a Renaissance commonplace, one that Shakespeare regularly takes up. There is for example Iago's "Nor poppy nor mandragora,/Nor all the drowsy syrops of the world/ Shall ever medicine thee to that sweet sleep/Which thou owedst yesterday", where the sibilants positively hiss with venom. There is too, Macbeth's desolating cry, "Macbeth hath murder'd sleep."

There is something desolating, too, about Leontes' cry, "What noise there, ho?" And, when he realises who has arrived, he will not – dare not? – speak directly to her:

> Away with that audacious lady! Antigonus,
> I charged thee that she should not come about me.
> I knew she would.

Antigonus: I told her so, my lord,
> On your displeasure's peril, and on mine,
> She should not visit you.

Leontes: What! Canst not rule her?

Paulina: From all dishonesty he can. In this –
> Unless he take the course that you have done:
> Commit me for committing honour – trust it,
> He shall not rule me.

From which we infer not merely that Paulina is fearlessly determined to tell the truth but that Leontes is scared of her. Why this should be comes out in a heart-stopping moment, when Leontes tries to deny his infant daughter's paternity. Paulina, he says, is a "callat" (lewd woman):

Of boundless tongue, who late hath beat her husband,
And now baits me! This brat is none of mine;
It is the issue of Polixenes.
Hence with it, and together with the dam
Commit them to the fire!

Paulina: It is yours;

For all his jeering at Antigonus' inability to rule his wife, Leontes'
fear of her is manifest in his refusal to speak to her, even, I suggest,
to look at her, as though he fears she will, like some gorgon figure,
strike him dumb. And so it more or less proves. For those three words
of hers "It is yours", require two strong stresses on "is yours" in
order to complete the pentameter line. Paulina's hammering
insistence on the truth, her steadfast, obdurate refusal to be cowed
by Leontes – we can imagine the others shrinking back in a mixture
of incredulity and awe at the power of her attack – is sealed when
she addresses "good goddess Nature, which hast made it [the infant]/
So like to him that got it, if thou hast/The ordering of the mind too,
'mongst all colours/No yellow in't, lest she suspect, as he does,/Her
children not her husband's." And *still* Leontes dare not speak to her
directly:

A gross hag!
And, losel, thou art worthy to be hanged,
Thou wilt not stay her tongue.

Antigonus: Hang all the husbands
That cannot do that feat, you'll leave yourself
Hardly one subject.

Leontes may call Antigonus a "losel", meaning a low scoundrel, but
Antigonus' reply makes plain that he's nothing of the sort. He's witty,
has taken courage from his wife's fearlessness to himself oppose the
king, and is, it seems plain, proud of her. And now Paulina, who for
the second time has invoked the goddess Nature, and is herself an
embodiment of such Nature, takes her leave without the baby, whom
Leontes commands Antigonus, in the most unnatural manner, to take
"To some remote and desert place" and there leave it "Without more
mercy, to its own protection." Antigonus agrees, but as he goes says

to the bundle in his arms: "blessing/Against this cruelty fight on thy side,/Poor thing, condemn'd to loss!" He, too, refuses to be cowed by Leontes.

This great scene has at its heart the inspiriting, indomitable Paulina, the character, let us remember, that Shakespeare has invented. Why? As I have already suggested, she has her antecedents, Rosalind and Beatrice among them. Moreover, in the comedies as a whole, women play dominant roles. The comic rhythm is concerned with the social fabric. The dance with which the early comedies conclude symbolises reconciliation and harmony, people coming together in a manner that shows them ready to take their parts in the social scheme. But in *The Winter's Tale* and *The Tempest*, dance occurs within rather than at the end of the play, and is succeeded by further disharmony. The reasons for this I will examine later. Here, I need to note that women's roles are in the last plays more circumscribed, more put upon than in the earlier comedies. This may have something to do with the fact that Elizabeth had been succeeded by James, whose behaviour and temperament included a strong misogynistic streak. He also used his power to make women do his bidding. In 1610 he forbade his cousin Arbella from marrying William Seymour, had Seymour shut in the Tower of London, and, after Seymour escaped, hoping that he and Arbella could elope to the continent and marry there, James saw to it that Arbella was caught and locked in the Tower for the rest of her life.

Women's functions in the later plays tell us much about the power of men to control and/or wreck the societies they seek to order, a matter explored in the great tragedies, where women are by and large the victims of such power, or seem to have no place. "My gracious silence, hail", Coriolanus says to his wife, Virgilia, thereby acknowledging the little real presence she has in his life. And Lady Macbeth, seeking to be the equal of her husband, has to "unsex" herself.

Paulina, Hermione, and the infant Perdita, are all subject to Leontes' diseased use of power. And at the juncture of the play we have reached there is no guarantee that any of them will survive. But Paulina is given an authority that overwhelms Leontes. As we have seen, he dare not speak to her, cannot bear even to look in her direction. She is a strong woman. And she is the only character in the play to bear a Christian name, Paulina, which derives from the male Paul.

St Paul took a dim view of marriage. "Art thou bound to a wife? seek not to be loosed. Art thou loosed from a wife? seek not a wife. But if thou marry, thou has not sinned; and if a virgin marry she hath not sinned. Nevertheless such shall have much trouble in the flesh." (1 *Corinthians* 7, 27-28). They that marry do well, they that refrain do better. Well, we might say, judging from the opening scenes of *The Winter's Tale*, there's a good deal to be said for Paul's argument, which also emphasised the need for women to be subservient to their husbands. But as soon as we note this, we can understand why the name as well as the nature of Paulina are so crucial to Shakespeare's play. For Paulina, the married woman, isn't subservient. On the contrary, by confronting and outwitting assumptions of the "rightness" of man's dominion over wife and, for that matter, society as a whole, her medicinal power shows itself. I am, she tells Leontes, "your physician". There are doctors aplenty in Shakespeare's plays, all of them male. None is as effective as Paulina.

*   *   *

But Paulina cannot persuade Leontes of the truth, any more than can the Oracle. The brief scene that opens Act III transports us from the infected air of Leontes' court to where "The climate's delicate, the air most sweet", where nature, in its "goodness", can be expected to utter the truth. Here, in other words, the Oracle is imagined as the utterance of Nature, or is an expression of that medicinal, curative power that Paulina arrogates to herself and that is elsewhere in the play associated with the gods, with heavenly powers, with all that lies beyond the merely human. It is for this reason that most commentators have felt that there is a strongly religious element in *The Winter's Tale* and that some have leaned towards a specifically Christian interpretation of the play, arguing that it is about sin and redemption through grace. There is some justification for this. Nevertheless, as Ernest Schanzer sensibly points out in his Introduction to the Penguin edition, "It is man's wishes, fears, and imaginings, rather than Fortune, Providence, or the gods, which are depicted as the prime movers of the play's events." The Oracle may propose, but Leontes disposes.

And so, in the long Act III, scene 2, we re-enter the infected air of Sicilia's court. Leontes puts Hermione on trial for "committing adultery with Polixenes, King of Bohemia, and conspiring with Camillo to take away the life of our sovereign lord the King". Hermione's declaration of innocence, in the great speeches that follow, have about them an almost Ciceronian dignity and calm, although to say that is to suggest that their rhetoric is somehow calculated, whereas Hermione's unhurried measures, her refusal of special pleading or histrionics – "For life, I prize it/As I weigh grief, which I would spare" – possess in equal measure *gravitas* and sweetness. Between them they make for an ungainsayable authority.

In an earlier, famous court scene, Portia had used forensic skills to outwit Shylock. She had been in control. But in this court scene it is Leontes who has the power and, so he would like to think, the authority to dispose of Hermione as he pleases. Yet he is repeatedly undone by Hermione's unshakeable composure. Seeking to prove his wife's complicity in some plot against him (the plot he has imagined), he says:

> You knew of his [Polixenes'] departure, as you know
> What you have underta'en to do in 's absence.

> *Hermione*: Sir,
> You speak a language that I understand not.
> My life stands in the level of your dreams,
> Which I'll lay down.

"I understand a fury in your words,/But not your words", Desdemona tells Othello as he grows wild in jealousy (*Othello* Act IV, scene 2, 32). Her own words mingle bewilderment and fear. (We should note that "But not your words" is an addition to be found in the first Quarto though it isn't in the Folio and is not always included by modern editors.) Hermione, though, shows no such fear – for herself, at all events. For her to tell Leontes that her life stands in the level of his dreams is as much as to say that she knows his distorted understanding of her makes him consider her a whore, or, more precisely, that she is the target of his murderous madness. We recall that in Act II, scene 3 Leontes had indeed said that "the harlot-king/ Is quite beyond mine arm, out of the blank/And level of my brain", where "blank" means the white bull's eye of the target used in gunnery practice, and "level" is both aim and range. We still speak of "levelling" a gun.

But note that single word "Sir"– it is so printed in the Folio and all editors follow suit, leaving the rest of the line blank. We have therefore to assume a held silence as Hermione gathers herself to speak. "Sir". It may be an imperious rebuke – how dare you impute such things to me – but if so anger is mastered by forbearance, even by pity for her husband. Her silence, to coin a phrase, speaks volumes, tells of her magnanimity, and, if I may risk saying so, of her instinctive readiness to feel for others, to entertain their point of view.

Not that Leontes, locked into the solipsistic world of his madness, notices this. And so, after his next rant of denunciation, which ends with him saying, "Look for no less than death", Hermione says again, "Sir", but this time wearily follows it with "Spare your threats!" and then:

> The bug which you would fright me with I seek.
> To me can life be no commodity:
> The crown and comfort of my life, your favour,
> I do give lost, for I do feel it gone,
> But know not how it went.

The last line may seem almost an afterthought. The sentence could easily have stopped at "gone". "But know not how it went" is, I think, murmured, almost to herself; it is the nearest she comes to giving way, and is for that reason intensely moving. For how *can* she know? How can anyone? But she rallies for one last time. She has, she tells him, lost all: her son is barred her, her husband has proclaimed her a harlot, and she herself:

> … hurried
> Here, to this place, i'th' open air, before
> I have got strength of limit. Now, my liege,
> Tell me what blessings I have here alive
> That I should fear to die.

There is no self-pity here, not even when she is telling him that so soon after childbirth she is scarcely fit to be brought "to this place". Her question gently but firmly scorns his threat of death. And whereas in the previous scene Paulina had discomposed, indeed routed Leontes by the implacable ferocity of her argument, he is here disadvantaged by his wife's composure, and by the largeness of spirit that even in her distress shows itself in her regard for him.

It is a spirit that the Oracle will vindicate. Hermione asks that "Apollo be my judge!" and a Lord – yet another not to be cowed by Leontes – says: "This your request/Is altogether just." The line break enforces a moment of hesitation. Will the Lord rule her request out of order? Does he look at Leontes before adding "Is altogether just"? If so, does he speak those words defiantly? Yes, to both, I think. And of course the Oracle proclaims Hermione innocent.

What follows does so at almost breakneck speed. Leontes, who it will be remembered himself sent for the Oracle's word (and so, in an important change from *Pandosto*, where it was Queen Bellaria who had appealed to the Oracle, takes on himself the responsibility of seeking out the truth) now denounces the news from Delphos as falsehood. Immediately, a servant enters with news of Mamillius' death, brought on, so he says, "with mere conceit and fear/Of the Queen's speed". Leontes replies: "Apollo's angry, and the heavens themselves/Do strike at my injustice." Hermione then faints and Paulina cries out:

> This news is mortal to the Queen: look down
> And see what death is doing.

Leontes: Take her hence.
> Her heart is but o'er charged; she will recover.
> I have too much believed mine own suspicion.
> Beseech you, tenderly apply to her
> Some remedies for life.

These are difficult moments to bring off successfully. It is, above all, astonishing that Leontes should so suddenly recover his senses. We have, I think, to understand that in this sad Tale, heavenly intervention is seen to play its part. Leontes' cry, "the heavens themselves/Do strike at my injustice" is borne out not merely by the news of his son's death but by Hermione's fainting fit and Paulina's cry "look down". In most productions I have seen she is made to address this remark to Leontes. In others she addresses the heavens.

"Look down" is then fearful, as though she is imploring the angry gods to go no further, yet aware that forces have been unleashed that cannot be controlled. But though characters in the play may see the terrible happenings as marks of divine displeasure, the fact remains that we the onlookers can see that they are caused by human action. And as Paulina is shortly to point this out to Leontes, it seems plain that it must be the king whom she commands to "look down." He is to see what he has done, what his actions have led to.

Leontes of course at first thinks he can simply and easily undo the consequences of his actions: "I'll reconcile me to Polixenes;/ New woo my Queen; recall the good Camillo." It is probably inevitable that an audience should laugh at the King's confidence in his ability to set to rights so many wrongs. And it is certainly astonishing that he should step so easily out of his madness, as though it were no more than an ill-fitting cloak that he's suddenly chosen to throw off. In part, it was, and we can now see that there was a degree of self-will about his wrapping himself in jealousy.

With Paulina's re-entry, however, the almost casual comedy of repentance falls away. She flays him with her anger, her determination to make him understand the horror of what he has done. His dream of repentance has after all quite forgot what Paulina calls "The casting forth to crows thy baby daughter", an act which would have caused "a devil/[to] shed water out of fire ere done 't." It also forgot the death of Mamillius, "whose honourable thoughts," Paulina now tells him, "cleft the heart/That could conceive a gross and foolish sire/ Blemished his gracious dam". But above all, "the Queen, the Queen,/ The sweet'st, dear'st creature's dead!"

I have to say that in all productions I have seen of *The Winter's Tale*, including some pretty dire ones, this moment never fails to appal, even though I know Hermione is not dead, that she is in Paulina's safe keeping. For in a sense she *is* dead. Leontes has killed the life he and Hermione had together and nothing can bring that back. Some things cannot be undone. And therefore, Paulina tells Leontes:

> ... betake thee
> To nothing but despair. A thousand knees,
> Ten thousand years together, naked, fasting,

Upon a barren mountain, and still winter
In storm perpetual, could not move the gods
To look that way thou wert.

Despair is the cardinal sin, placing the person who falls into it beyond the possibility of God's grace. It was despair that finally sent Faustus to hell. Paulina may have no authority to so condemn Leontes, but her words have a terrifying, almost Jesuitical power of suggestion. And in her refusal to recognise Leontes as in any way deserving of respect – she addresses him by the second-person singular, "*thou* tyrant" "*thee*", "*thou* wert" (my emphases) – she not only strips away his authority, she places him on a level that is below human consideration.

Leontes accepts the justice of her anger – "Go on, go on:/Thou canst not speak too much" – but "A Lord" speaks up for moderation, as Lords in this play so regularly do. The king may be infected but his court is singularly free from taint and this, I think, has to be read as Shakespeare's endorsement of ideals and values associated with *noblesse oblige*: The fact that the Lord is unnamed reinforces this. Any Lord can be expected to say what this one does, which is to urge Paulina to desist: "Howe'er the business goes, you have made fault/ I' th' boldness of your speech."

Paulina accepts the rebuke: "he is touched/To th' noble heart", she says, and adds:

Do not receive affliction
At my petition, I beseech you; rather
Let me be punished, that have minded you
Of what you should forget.

The untouchable Leontes has been "touched". It makes good sense for Paulina after this to step towards the king, whom we can assume to be prostrate, and place a hand on his shoulder as she says "I beseech you". But note she now gives him back his authority: no longer is he "thee" but "you". Her storm is nearly played out. "Take your patience to you," she tells him, "And I'll say nothing."

Leontes, wiser now than when he thought repentance could be slipped into as easily as a pair of new shoes, knows that he must learn to face what he has done. Hence, his remark to Paulina that,

"Thou didst speak but well/When most the truth; which I receive much better/Than to be pitied of thee." And the scene ends with him asking Paulina to conduct him into the presence of his dead son and wife: "lead me to these sorrows." As so often, the line break is important.* It enacts a pause before Leontes can utter the phrase that truly acknowledges what he himself has brought about: "these sorrows."

*   *   *

But we are not yet done with sorrows. Scene 3 opens with Antigonus, the infant in his arms, ashore on Bohemia's coast. (Which, yes, had no seashore.) A storm threatens and the mariner accompanying Antigonus wants to get away as fast as possible. "The heavens," he says, "are angry,/And frown upon 's." Antigonus' reply makes plain that the heavens are invoked as no casual metonym: "Their sacred wills be done!" Once more, the gods seems to be intervening. Not only that: Antigonus recounts to the "poor babe" his dream of the previous night, when Hermione appeared to him "in pure white robes,/Like very sanctity," to entreat him that "for the babe/is counted lost for ever, Perdita/I prithee, call't." Moreover, the spirit tells him, "For this ungentle business,/Put on thee by my lord, thou ne'er shalt see/Thy wife Paulina more." Antigonus is therefore, we sense, to become one more victim of Leontes' madness. He certainly believes that, as Hermione's spirit has visited him, she must be dead, her guilt having been proved by the Oracle. It is therefore proper to leave Perdita in Bohemia, "this being indeed the issue/Of King Polixenes ... its right father."

Yet this bluff, plain-speaking man bewildered out of certainty, his conscience troubled, is capable of great tenderness. He may think Polixenes the baby's father, but this is not to condemn it:

> Blossom, speed thee well!
> There lie, and there thy character; there these,
> Which may, if fortune please, both breed thee, pretty,
> And still rest thine. The storm begins. Poor wretch,

---

* This line break is not in the Penguin edition but is present in all other major editions of the play, and is clearly of importance.

That for thy mother's fault art thus exposed
To loss and what may follow! Weep I cannot,
But my heart bleeds; and most accursed am I
To be by oath enjoined to this.

Antigonus is a man of honour. As such, he must stay true to the oath he swore when, following Paulina's exit in Act II, scene 3, Leontes tried to re-assert his authority, and vowed to have Hermione's infant burnt. The king relents only to the extent of requiring Antigonus to "adventure/To save this brat's life." "I'll pawn the little blood which I have left/To save the innocent" Antigonus replies, and is made to swear by Leontes' sword that he will do the king's bidding. "I will, my lord" the old man says, at which point he must touch the sword at the hilt, where it forms a cross. The oath he has sworn is therefore a sacred one. That he should refer to the infant as "innocent" is perhaps not so much because he disbelieves the charge against Hermione as because, contrary to orthodox Christian belief, he refuses to accept that the infant is ineluctably tainted by her mother's sin. Not for nothing, we may reflect, is he Paulina's husband. Now, alone with Perdita, and knowing, as he thinks, that Hermione has been found guilty, he still calls Perdita "Blossom", "pretty", though she is also a "poor wretch,/That for thy mother's fault art thus exposed/To loss." This requires further comment.

When Dickens came to write *Bleak House* he took as heroine a girl, Esther Summerson, who was the illegitimate daughter of a woman forced to give up her up. Esther is reared as an orphan by her godmother who, on the occasion of Esther's birthday, tells the little girl, "Your mother, Esther, is your disgrace, and you were hers … For yourself, unfortunate girl, orphaned and degraded from the first of these evil anniversaries, pray daily that the sins of others be not visited upon your head, according to what is written." The godmother here alludes to the *Old Testament*, specifically the book of *Numbers*: "The Lord is slow to anger, and plenteous in mercy, forgiving iniquity and transgression, and that will by no means clear the guilty; visiting the iniquity of the fathers upon the children, upon the third and upon the fourth generation." (14-18) The Church taught that in this context, iniquity referred to the sin of illegitimacy. As a small boy in the late 1940s I can recall whispering campaigns conducted in the school playground, and elsewhere, against a boy who was, we understood "a bastard", and who seemed as a result irredeemably tainted, as Esther thinks herself tainted, endlessly shadowed by her "iniquity".

I draw attention to these matters because to scant them is to undervalue Antigonus' decency. His heart does battle with his head, with the 'knowledge' that Perdita can in any way inherit her mother's sin. "Weep I cannot". He does not refrain from tears because he is a man but because he wants to think that justice is being done. "But my heart bleeds." The line break between the two statements attests to the grieved split in himself, one that makes him, as he feels, "accursed". There is no way back for him.

3

Bohemia: A New World?

Exit, pursued by a bear. This famous stage direction, which unlike many is to be found in the Folio, has prompted much editorial comment. Did Shakespeare's company have access to a real bear? Perhaps, because there was a bear-pit at Southwark, hard by the Globe. White bears were used to draw a chariot in Ben Jonson's *Masque of Oberon*, 1611. Alternatively, one of the actors may simply have wrapped himself in a bear skin and chased Antigonus off stage. But why? Is the moment intended to be tragic or comic, frightening or absurd? The answer, I think, is any or all of these things. For this is the moment of transition, almost of transformation, of one world to another, not merely Sicilia to Bohemia, but court to country, night to day, winter to spring: not literally, in all cases, but with a sense that the world of the play is now turning over.

The idea of transformation is virtually as old as drama itself, and is located either in a person who is 'discovered' not to be a beggar but a prince, or, as theatre moves indoors, becomes increasingly associated with stage magic, familiar to us still in pantomime. (Apple to wasp, pumpkin to coach.) By 1610/11 masques were increasingly making use of stage machinery to engineer transformations. That Shakespeare and his company were familiar with masque is evident in *The Tempest*, where Prospero conjures up the masquers to celebrate Miranda's forthcoming marriage to Ferdinand (Act IV, scene 1). We can imagine Prospero waving his wand to begin the show. The wand is in this instance a variant on the slapstick which Columbine used in the 16th century Italian form of drama, *Commedia dell' Arte* – literally slapping his stick on the stage floor – in order to signal a moment of change. (It sent a message to stagehands that they had minutes to set in motion whatever machinery brought that change about.) And, as in *The Tempest* Prospero conjures up a masque, so, too, in *The Winter's Tale*, there are masque-like dances in Act IV, scene 4, which we shall come to in due course, and which undoubtedly point to and exploit contemporary fascination with this new form of drama. But at this moment of Antigonus' departure, the bear chasing him off stage seems no more than a tongue-in-cheek allusion to the show of masque.

But then we suddenly become aware of a shepherd. I emphasise this because I want to draw attention to the fact that there is no fanfare to herald this arrival – how could there be? – and that, assuming our eyes have been following Antigonus' precipitate exit, we are unlikely to be aware of the Shepherd's presence until he begins to speak. It is therefore of the utmost importance that in the Folio there is no stage direction to tell us of his entry. It is as if he is an emanation of some new spirit. Though we cannot always know the reasons for the Folio's comparative reluctance to give stage directions, here at least it seems entirely proper. A transformation is taking place, but not one that announces itself. No slapstick. No thunder. This moment of transformation is entirely unemphatic. And with this in mind, I want to consider some lines in the American poet William Carlos Williams' poem 'Spring and All': "Lifeless in appearance, sluggish/dazed spring approaches". The spring signals its imminent coming in the shape of new growths:

> But now the stark dignity of
> entrance Still, the profound change
> has come upon them: rooted, they
> grip down and begin to awaken

There is no full stop at the end of the poem. Awakening is a process.

Williams' words can be applied point by point to this moment in *The Winter's Tale*. But above all, the sense of new growth being paradoxically "lifeless in appearance" is surely close to the feeling of life-out-of-death which Act III, scene 3 generates: of uncertain endings, hesitant beginnings. The old world doesn't disappear in some cataclysmic moment of horror, but is figured as an old man being chased by a bear. The new doesn't arrive in a blaze of trumpets but with the manifestation on stage of a shepherd. Not a man of stark dignity, to be sure, but one who for all that heralds profound change.

I have read schematic interpretations of this play which require the Shepherd to be a kind of surrogate Christ figure, an emblem of humility embodying forgiveness, love and assurance of a better future. I disagree. To be sure, Christ is often imaged as the good shepherd carrying a sheep on his back, but good man though we will discover this shepherd undoubtedly to be, his opening words make plain that his concern for now is with daily business. This shepherd is irreducibly of the earth, is stubbornly matter-of-fact:

> I would there were no age between ten and three-and-
> twenty, or that youth would sleep out the rest: for there is
> nothing in the between but getting wenches with child,
> wronging the ancientry, stealing, fighting ... They have
> scared away two of my best sheep ...

The rural life is no idyll, no golden pastoral.

Then the old man stumbles across the bundle Antigonus has left and finds "A very pretty barne. A boy or a child, I wonder?" This distinction, between boy and "child", is one that survives to this day in rural Greece, where, however, offspring are either 'daughters' or 'children'. In such communities a daughter spells trouble. (There is the matter of dowry.) But it is more troubling than that, even. The son as child is acknowledged fruit of the loins. A daughter has no such claim. Though he reverses the terms, the shepherd instinctively reveals that he thinks the same way. A boy is a more distinct entity than a mere child.

Yet the dismissive "child" does not attest to his true feelings. Nor does his guess that she is the product of "some behind-door-work" debar her from his sympathy. She may be illegitimate, may be evidence in the flesh of that "getting wenches with child" of which he has just been grumbling, but as "they were warmer that got this than the poor thing is here. I'll take it up for pity."

At which point, the Folio tells us, *Enter Clowne*. The Clown is the Shepherd's son, and his being so typed undoubtedly indicates his role. But this is not to say that he is to be thought of as a mere bumpkin. Costard the Clown of *Love's Labours Lost* is one of that play's sources of true, earthy, wit. But in *The Winter's Tale,* Shepherd and Clown – they have no other, individualising names – take on what might be called 'typical' roles. And as these are linked to the meaning of pastoral, I will reserve further comment on these roles until a later moment. Here, I want to note that the Shepherd's son tells his father, and us, of the fate of the mariners and Antigonus. All are lost, the former in a tempest at sea, the latter grotesquely killed and eaten. "Heavy matters" the Shepherd says, and then he utters the play's most famous words: "Now bless thyself: thou met'st with things dying, I with things new-born." We might perhaps expect that it would be more appropriate for these meetings to be reversed: the older man, the Shepherd, to witness death, his son to discover Perdita. But no: sluggish/dazed spring approaches. The transition is not smooth.

It remains only for the two to discover the gold Antigonus has left with Perdita and to pronounce it "fairy gold", and for the Clown to tell his father that, "You're a made old man. If the sins of your youth are forgiven you, you're well to live" (he calls his father "You", the Shepherd says "thee" and "thou" when talking to his son: even here the proprieties are maintained) and the first great movement of the play is done. What wealth Perdita brings to the world into which she has been introduced we are now to discover.

*   *   *

Enter Time, the Chorus.

> I that please some, try all; both joy and terror
> Of good and bad; that makes and unfolds error,
> Now take upon me, in the name of Time,
> To use my wings. Impute it not a crime
> To me or my swift passage, that I slide
> O'er sixteen years ...

Time is used to bridge the gap between the world we have left and the Bohemian world we are now to meet. In his great essay on 'Father Time' in *Studies in Iconology*, Erwin Panofsky points out that the figure to be found in much Renaissance and Baroque art has a complex history, half western and half oriental, and that Time may act as "a Destroyer, or as a Revealer, or as a universal and inexorable power which through a cycle of procreation and destruction causes what may be called cosmic continuity: 'thou nursest all and murder'st all that are', to speak in Shakespeare's words." These particular words come from 'The Rape of Lucrece', where Time is figured as that which brings all to fruition, whether good or bad. Time has a similar agency in *The Winter's Tale*. But Time here also acts as Revealer, unfolder of error. As Panofsky notes, Father Time is often imaged as vindicating the virtuous and justifying innocence. So it will prove in Shakespeare's play. And although in this interlude, which is what Act IV, scene 1 amounts to, Time fills the audience in on the essential details of what has happened during the 16 years we are to flip over, Time's other functions will also be assumed by theatre-goers who presumably see before them an actor dressed in long robes, clutching a scythe (Time the destroyer, the reaper of men) and holding a mirror, which according to Panofsky is used either to indicate "the gradual decay of health and beauty" (think how often it is so used in the *Sonnets*) or to confront people with the truth, show them what otherwise they could not see, as the Chorus does when he says: "I turn my glass, and give my scene such growing/As you had slept between."

There used to be some critical consternation that in creating this 16 year gap Shakespeare should so cavalierly ignore the Unities of time, place, and action. I imagine that especially since the advent of film such objections have died away. For a period of the 1930s and 1940s, Hollywood regularly made use of racing train wheels on which were superimposed the turning pages of a calendar in order to indicate a shift of locale and time. Shakespeare's Time performs a similar function. Besides, as Dr Johnson wonderfully said, when he dismissed the criticism that in *Antony and Cleopatra* Shakespeare too often switched between Egypt and Rome, we know perfectly well that the play takes place upon the stage.

Yet Time does alert us to the movement of the play, which is not merely from one place to another, or over a specific period but, as Panofksy says, one that testifies to "cosmic continuity." Here, then, it will help to invoke the work of the American aesthetic philosopher, Susanne Langer. In her great work, *Feeling and Form*, Langer has a section on "The Great Dramatic Forms", divided into what she calls "The Comic Rhythm" and "The Tragic Rhythm". Her arguments, which are worked out at some length, are far too subtle to be fairly reproduced in a few sentences, but at the risk of unfairly simplifying, I will note that for her the "Tragic Rhythm" includes the requirement that the protagonist "grows mentally, emotionally, or morally, by the demand of the action, which he himself initiated, to the complete exhaustion of his powers, the limits of his possible development." This is only partly true of Leontes. He certainly initiated the action which, by the end of Act III, has brought him to the "exhaustion of his powers." Yet further development may not be beyond him, and if this is so it may be that he is not the fully tragic figure of Langer's definition.

To speculate in this manner is of course to return us to the question with which I opened my study. What kind of a play is *The Winter's Tale*? Is it perhaps better considered as obeying the "Comic Rhythm"? Here is Langer:

> [Comedy] is at once religious and ribald, knowing and defiant, social and freakishly individual. The illusion of life which the comic poet creates is the oncoming future fraught with dangers and opportunities, that is, with physical or social events occurring by chance and building up the coincidences with which individuals cope according to their lights. This ineluctable future – ineluctable because its countless factors are beyond human knowledge and control – is Fortune ... the immediate sense of life is the underlying feeling of comedy, and dictates its rhythmically structured unity, that is to say its organic form.
>
> Comedy is an art form that arises naturally wherever people are gathered to celebrate life. in spring festivals, triumphs, birthdays, weddings, or initiations. For it expresses the elementary strains and resolutions of animate nature, the animal drives that persist even in human nature, the delight man takes in his special mental gifts that makes him the lord of creation; it is an image of human vitality holding its own in the world amid the surprises of unplanned coincidence.

The phrase "unplanned coincidence" may give us pause, but Langer has earlier suggested that the comic rhythm, its symbolic pattern, is evidence of what she calls man's "brainy opportunism in face of an essentially dreadful universe." (Susanne K. Langer, *Feeling and Form: A Theory of Art*, London, 1953. See esp. Chap. 18 and 19.)

Langer writes as a humanist and, to repeat a point made earlier, many commentators have felt that in common with other of the late plays *The Winter's Tale* is an essentially religious play, or that it has at least a deep intuitive awareness of the presence of forces acting on human beings that, in Langer's words, are "beyond human knowledge or control", but are nevertheless, and *pace* humanist beliefs, purposive. To put the matter this way is inevitably to recall Hamlet's words: "There is a destiny that shapes our ends,/Rough hew them how we will." Yet even Hamlet's destiny is not determined by forces he is entirely powerless to oppose. Or rather, those 'forces' are located in human action, most of which is explicable. Certainly nothing in any of the tragedies is as inexplicable as Leontes' mad jealousy, not even Lear's taking leave of his senses. Wilson Knight calls Leontes' madness "evil", but this explains nothing, It certainly does not answer the questions, *how* and *why* Leontes' jealousy comes about.

But this jealousy and the terrible sequence of events it sets in motion are real enough. Now, with Time as Chorus to open the door into a new world, we seem to bid farewell to the male dominated tragic rhythm of the play's opening acts and step into one associated with spring, Proserpine, Persephone, Primavera – call the spirit what you will – that image of the year's rebirth whose incarnation is the "Blossom" Antigonus had, it feels, planted on Bohemia's shore. At which moment the comic rhythm, however tentatively, begins to take over. And at the same time, as Sicilia is replaced by Bohemia, we step from court life to pastoral.

There is, however, nothing schematic about this, let alone any simple opposition of infection and purity. Shakespeare is well aware of the dream of pastoral, of an Edenic world, but he is far from believing in its realisation here, on this bank and shoal of time. When, at the beginning of *As You Like It*, we hear of the skullduggery that has led to a Duke's banishment from court, we are told of the rumour that he and his party "fleet the time carelessly, as they did in the golden world." But we are to discover that the world of Arden is tarnished by far more than "winter and rough weather." So with Bohemia.

4

Pastoral and Anti-Pastoral

Act IV scene 2 is taken up with a conversation between Polixenes and the self-exiled Camillo, eager to see his own country once more. Leontes, "the penitent King, my master, hath sent for me; to whose feeling sorrows I might be some allay", he tells Polixenes. But Polixenes begs him to stay a while longer. Why? – because he is worried about his son, who is spending too much time at "the house of a most homely shepherd." Camillo has heard of such a man. He has also heard that he has "a daughter of most rare note." "Yes," Polixenes, says, "but, I fear, the angle that plucks our son thither." He then prevails on Camillo to accompany him in disguise, to "have some question with the shepherd." "The angle". We can scarcely hear Polixenes use that term without uneasily recalling Leontes' charge that many a man has had "his pond fished by his next neighbour", although there the male neighbour was the active one, here the shepherd's daughter is figured as the active agent that draws the king's son, "plucks [him] thither."

The two men exit and we naturally expect to see next the Shepherd and his daughter. For this is how Shakespeare so often works, especially at the beginning of plays, and this is, if not the opening of the play, a new beginning. We hear of something striking about certain characters, who then appear, either to confirm or confute what has been said. But not here. Instead, *Enter Autolycus Singing*: "When daffodils begin to peer,/With heigh, the doxy over the dale." What Autolycus sings is a ballad about earthy pleasures, including drinking and whoring.* He is shabbily, even raggedly dressed. "I have served Prince Florizel," he tells us, "and in my time wore three-pile; but now I am out of service." He then sings again:

* See over page.

> If tinkers may have leave to live,
>   And bear the sow-skin budget,
> Then my account I well may give,
>   And in the stocks avouch it.

He means that should he be arrested for vagabondage, he will claim to be a tinker, for at least, like a tinker, he has a pigskin wallet. I imagine at this point he will show the audience that his is empty. Tinkers, it should be said, those tradesmen who wandered from place to place in search of work, had a reputation for being tale-tellers. Naturally, because they brought stories of one place to another, usually well rehearsed and embroidered, it was part of their attraction. They were exotic, and they were associated with a kind of buoyant, raffish self-sufficiency. "Merry as a tinker" was a phrase still in use when I was a boy, likewise "a little tinker", used of impish children, and although Autolycus isn't a tinker – his trade, he tells us, is in stealing sheets – he has the resilience and ready wit associated with them.

And Shakespeare invented him. True, in Greene's *Pandosto* there is a character called Capnio who is servant to Dorastus (Florizel in *The Winter's Tale*), but for all this faint foreshadowing of Shakespeare's character, Autolycus is, essentially, an original. His part would have been played by Robert Armin, who had joined the King's Company some 10 years earlier, and who was a regular favourite with the Globe's audiences as comic actor and singer. There is ample opportunity in *The Winter's Tale* for Armin to show off his skills, and this self-styled "snapper-up of unconsidered trifles" soon has a chance to show his mettle. For the Clown now enters, clutching a bag of money and worrying to himself about what he's to buy "for our sheep-shearing feast." And as a fool and his money are soon parted, it takes Autolycus little time to get his hands on the Clown's.

---

* "Doxy", like the word "aunts" which Autolycus uses in the same song ("summer songs for me and my aunts/While we lie tumbling in the hay") implies a woman who sells her sexual favours, though it would be wrong to conclude that she is a prostitute in the modern sense. She is more like the "scrubber" about whom the jazz singer George Melly writes in his autobiography, *Owning Up*, the kind of woman who knows the men she goes with and has half-affectionate, half-professional relationships with them. Like Autolycus, a doxy is someone who has to find a way to survive in a harsh world and to get as much fun as she can while doing it.

"If the springe hold, the cock's mine", he says. He means that he will use his wit as a trap to catch this particular bird. (Probably a woodcock, conventionally thought a stupid bird.) This reference to poaching tells us of Autolycus' readiness to walk on the wild side of the law. And now we watch as, pretending to have been robbed and beaten, he gets the Clown to help him to his feet and, as the Clown does so, Autolycus picks his pocket, saying, in ostensible reference to the other man's help, "You ha' done me a charitable office."

No doubt he will 'mug' at the audience as he says these words, perhaps wink, probably pat his pocket where the Clown's money now rests. At which point the Clown good-heartedly asks him. "Dost lack any money? I have a little money for thee."

> *Autolycus:* No, good, sweet sir; no, I beseech you, sir, I have a
> kinsman not past three-quarters of a mile hence, unto
> whom I was going.

We can assume that as he speaks Autolycus holds the Clown so as to prevent him from reaching into his pocket and discovering his loss. Self-interest parodies the embrace of true hospitality. It is funny, but it is also discomposing. Autolycus the rogue, living the only way he knows how, is quite ready to exploit others, a matter about which he has no qualms.

At the end of the scene he sings again:

> Jog on, jog on, the footpath way,
> And merrily hent the stile-a:
> A merry heart goes all the day,
> Your sad tires in a mile-a.

"Simply the thing I am shall make me live". The words of Parolles, the clown in *All's Well That Ends Well*, apply equally well to Autolycus. He is the very image of self-sufficiency, living by his wits, troublingly attractive because entirely amoral, and a surely familiar type to any audience in any circumstance. That Shakespeare should choose to introduce us to this character as a way into the rural life makes plain that we can be under no illusion that such a life offers an uncontaminated vision of some "golden world".

Pastoral is, in other words, a conservative vision, not merely because it looks back to some previous, usually unspecified, moment of human history when all had been well with human affairs, but because it imagines these affairs as reliably harmonious or, if disturbed, then re-established along harmonious lines once whatever threatens a disturbance is removed. The ultimate pastoral is, of course, Eden before the Fall. And this is a tragic pastoral because the serpent's tempting of Eve brings about the end of Eden. But most pastoral is anti-tragic. The intruder is repelled. In *The Winter's Tale*, however, it is not merely Autolycus who acts as a potentially disruptive force, and who, just because he *isn't* an intruder, challenges the sentimentality of a pastoral vision that has no room for unregenerate human nature. Far more threatening is the figure of Polixenes, whose capacity to break up the world into which he intrudes will become evident as the play proceeds. His actions give the lie to any hope that the rural scene can be held inviolate against intrusive power.

*   *   *

But this is to anticipate. First, we have the pastoral scene in all its innocent beauty. For it is now that Perdita finally makes her appearance. She is one of a pastoral group that includes, as well as Polixenes and Camillo in disguise, the Shepherd, Clown, and other shepherds and shepherdesses, identified in the Folio as Mopsa and Dorcas, names that belong to the artificial world of pastoral. Here, then, we need to note the extraordinary blend that Shakespeare manages in this scene, between the artifice of pastoral convention and the flesh-and-blood reality of his characters and their relationships. Act IV, scene 4 of *The Winter's Tale* is one of the greatest pieces of dramatic writing I know.

The setting is the sheep-shearing feast of which the Clown has already spoken. And as Florizel's opening words make plain, Perdita has dressed for her role in the feast:

> These your unusual weeds to each part of you
> Does give a life: no shepherdess, but Flora
> Peering in April's front.

"Unusual weeds." Perdita is not in her customary shepherdess costume. Moreover she gives an especial grace to the costume she now wears. They and the garlands she must have around her neck and perhaps her waist, define her as 'Flora', goddess of fertility and flowers, whose connection to Persephone and her mother, Ceres, is through rituals that celebrate the (re)birth of the year. And as Florizel's name sufficiently indicates, he, too, is part of this new, fresh world. He is also, of course, a king's son, as Perdita is ostensibly a shepherd's daughter. What Shakespeare's audience would there have seen are two presumably young male actors, one pretending to be a girl who is pretending not to be a shepherdess but a minor deity, the other a young prince who is pretending to be a rustic character called Doricles. And as Shakespeare's audience would very well know, the Greek word Doric implied not merely rural but uncouth. And what the audience would then have realised is that at this point the play fuses together a specifically English tradition of rural festivity with a new dramatic form, masque, to which I have already made reference, and which was beginning to find favour under James. This needs some teasing out.

*   *   *

First, the sheep-shearing feast itself. Such feasts, which were built into the rural year, took place late in June, although as the Arden editor points out, Shakespeare seems to place the feast rather later in the year. (Or so the reference at line 79 in IV, scene 4 to "the year growing ancient" may suggest, and yet the scene feels to have an early summer setting. Shakespeare is, I think, deliberately vague about this: it is all summer.) The feasts were of various degrees of elaborateness, but even the meanest required shepherds to wear posies in their caps, exchange flowers with shepherdesses (including lavender and rosemary), involved music, drinking, eating and dancing – paying for the food and drink and musicians might cost a good deal – and usually included the election of a king and queen from among the company. Writing rather more than a hundred years after Shakespeare's play, Henry Bourne testified to the continuing importance of the feast:

> The Feast of Sheep-Shearing is generally a time of mirth and joy, and more than ordinary Hospitality, for on the Day they begin to sheer their Sheep, they provide a plentiful Dinner for

the Sheerers, and for their Friends who come to visit them on that Occasion; a Table also, if the Weather permit, is spread in the open Village, for the young People and the Children.

(Antiquatates Vulgares: or, the Antiquities of the Common People)

Bourne was writing in 1725. One hundred and fifty years after that, Thomas Hardy depicts a similar feast in *Far From the Madding Crowd*. Clearly, we are dealing here with a most important event in the rural calendar, and one in which, we must note, hospitality and entertainment are as central as ever they were in the court customs to which we are introduced at the play's outset.

But in referring to Perdita as Flora, Florizel identifies her with masque, and the presence of a masque element is evident not merely from the dance of Shepherds and Shepherdesses, at line 168, but, later, at line 343, *Here a Dance of Twelve Satyrs*. (In Greek mythology, satyrs were followers of Dionysus: grotesque creatures, part human, part beast: lustful, fond of revelry.) The specific point of this I will come to in due course; here, it is enough to note that by means of such references, Shakespeare deepens what might be called the scene's cultural politics. For masque is a courtly form of drama, and in its greatest exponent, Ben Jonson, draws on classical learning in order to provide its themes with ultimate authority. By 1611 Jonson had established an unrivalled position as author of, among others, the *Masque of Blacknesse* (1605), *The Masque of Beautie* (1608) and, perhaps most important for us, *Hymenaei* (1606), the "Masque of Union", written for the marriage of the young Earl of Essex to Frances Howard, daughter of the Earl of Suffolk. It was with the *Hymenaei* specifically in mind that Jonson set out his views of what the masque as an art form should be about. The function of masque, he says, is to give permanent expression of certain values, and this it does by making:

the most royall Princes, and greatest persons (who are commonly the presenters of these actions) not only studious of riches, and magnificence in the outward celebration, or shew; (which rightly becomes them) but curious after the most high, and heartie invention, to furnish the inward parts (and those grounded upon antiquitie, and solid learnings) which, though their voyce be taught to sound to present occasions,

their sense, or doth, or should always lay hold on more remov'd
mysteries.

I have taken this from an essay in *The Renaissance Imagination:
Essays and Lectures* by D.J. Gordon (edited by Stephen Orgel), which
is one of the greatest collections of essays ever on its chosen subject.
Gordon's writings on the masque in particular have an unsurpassable
authority and are recommended to anyone who wishes to enquire
into the form. Courtiers did not act on the public stage. But they did
take part in masques, which were after all private entertainments for
and about them as individuals and as types. Hence, in *The Winter's
Tale* we see a prince taking part in a feast which is also a kind of
masque, in which he plays a shepherd, Doricles, a lowly lover to
Flora. And as the masque, like pastoral, takes for its social vision the
blessed state of reconciliation between all elements of society, so
shepherds and court have to be brought together in a harmony
depicted through dance. The dance is absent from Jonson's exactly
contemporary poem, 'To Penshurst', but in other respects the poem
images an ideal of harmony, of social mutuality, between the great
family, the Sidneys, and those who work the surrounding land:

> And though thy walls be built of country stone,
> They're reared with no man's ruin, no man's groan,
> There's none, that dwell around them, wish them down,
> But all come in, the farmer and the clown:
> And no one empty-handed, to salute
> Thy lord, and lady, though they have no suit ...

Farmer and clown rejoice in bringing fruit to the great house which
stands open to receive them. Hospitality goes hand in hand with this
ideal of social cohesion, with the acceptance of social order. This is
the essential pastoral vision.

But in Act IV, scene 4 of our play the threat of disharmony hangs
over the feast, at all events in Perdita's fearful imagination:

> Even now I tremble
> To think your father by some accident
> Should pass this way, as you did. O, the Fates!
> How would he look to see his work, so noble,
> Vilely bound up?

Words such as these do, I am certain, indicate how different was the kind of audience for whom Shakespeare principally wrote, from the courtly spectators at Jonson's masques. Jonson could present social harmony as an achieved condition; but Perdita voices a more realistic view of the matter.

Florizel can afford to be more relaxed. "Apprehend/Nothing but jollity", he tells the girl, then playfully mentions many god-like metamorphoses:

> Jupiter
> Became a bull, and bellowed; the green Neptune
> A ram, and bleated; and the fire-robed god,
> Golden Apollo, a poor humble swain,
> As I seem now.

Then, remembering god-like rapes, he distances himself from such disguises: "my desires/Run not before mine honour, nor my lusts/Burn hotter than my faith."

But Perdita remains unconvinced, less of his vow of chastity than of his ability to remain steadfast in face of his father's likely fury. At the very least this suggests that, while Polixenes' reputation may not have gone before him, marriage of peasant and prince is out of the question. Social harmony is achieved, not by people transgressing social bounds, but by their willingness to remain within them. On this, masque and pastoral agree. Once again, therefore, Florizel tries to reassure her: "I cannot be/Mine own, nor anything to any, if/I be not thine. To this I am most constant". Then, having commanded her to "Lift up your countenance" for the approaching guests, he says, "Address yourself to entertain them sprightly."

His words are echoed and built on by the Shepherd, recalling how his "old wife" would take upon herself the duties of hospitality; how she:

> … welcomed all, served all;
> Would sing her song and dance her turn …
> > You are retired,
> As if you were a feasted one and not
> The hostess of the meeting. Pray you, bid
> These unknown friends to 's welcome, for it is
> A way to make us better friends, more known.

The "unknown friends" are of course the disguised Polixenes and Camillo, and there is a keen irony in the Shepherd's thinking that making them welcome will guarantee that they become more bound into the social group. But notice how in requiring Perdita to be the hostess of the meeting, the shepherd echoes Hermione's calling herself "your kind hostess", where to repeat, "kind" means "warm-hearted", "proper, rightful", and "of the nature of". It is of Hermione's nature to be the embodiment of hospitality and so it will prove with Perdita. Time moves on but time is also cyclic, as the feast the company is celebrating lets us know.

Perdita, however, embodies hospitality in a different way from her mother. "Mistress o' th' Feast" the Shepherd dubs her, and as this feast has to do with fruitfulness and the natural procession of the seasons, Perdita, having welcomed first Polixenes and then Camillo, takes flowers from her companion, Dorcas, and gives her new "friends":

> ... rosemary and rue; these keep
> Seeming and savour all the winter long:
> Grace and remembrance be to you both,
> And welcome to our shearing!

Polixenes replies gracefully enough that her gifts "fit our ages/With flowers of winter." What then follows is the passage of arms between them on nature versus nurture, in which each takes the position that will find them out.

Perdita tells Polixenes that although the fairest flowers of the season are "gillyvors", some call them "Nature's bastards; of that kind/Our rustic garden's barren, and I care not/To get slips of them." Why not, Polixenes asks. Because, she says, "There is an art which in their piedness shares/With great creating Nature." She doesn't know it, but she is echoing the very words with which Paulina argued for the propriety of her, Perdita's, own birth. Paulina, we remember, insisted that the taint of bastardy was not to be visited on the infant, that "good goddess Nature" had made Perdita so like Leontes as to leave no doubt about her paternity.

But Polixenes argues for the improvements that art can make to nature by means of grafting. And it is all Nature, he says, meaning, it is all according to laws we should not question. For:

43

> ... Nature is made better by no mean
> But Nature makes that mean; so over that art
> Which you say adds to Nature is an art
> That Nature makes. You see, sweet maid, we marry
> A gentler scion to the wildest stock,
> And make conceive a bark of baser kind
> By bud of nobler race. This is an art
> Which does mend Nature – change it, rather – but
> The art itself is Nature.

Perdita: So it is.

Polixenes: Then make your garden rich in gillyvors,
               And do not call them bastards.

Polixenes' speech has about it a degree of complacent condescension that we can imagine getting under Perdita's skin. This isn't to say that his argument lacks persuasiveness, but that phrase "sweet maid" is inviting her to consider his superior wisdom, a knowledge of the world that puts her ignorance to shame. And of course it glitters with proleptic irony: "we marry/A gentler scion to the wildest stock." At the end of *Pericles*, *Prince of Tyre*, Lysimachus says of Marina, of whose parentage he is unaware:

> She's such a one that, were I well assur'd
> Came of gentle kind and noble stock,
> I'd wish no better choice, and think me rarely wed.
>   (Act V, scene 1, 66-8)

Polixenes voices no such caution. For him, grafting as an art to "mend" or, he corrects himself, "change" nature, is tantamount to envisaging an ideal commonwealth, a blending of gentle and wild, base and noble. And the terms he uses inevitably apply both to the natural and human. "Scion" means both "twig, shoot" and "a heir, a descendant; a younger member of a noble family."

But Perdita is unpersuaded: "I'll not put/The dibble in earth to set one slip of them". What we might call her instinctive feeling for the purity of stock we have also to register as another unconscious irony, because it signifies a rejection of the very marriage that she and Florizel are about to enter into. After all, she knows he is a gentler scion and believes herself to be of baser stock. True, she adroitly turns the argument:

> No more than, were I painted, I would wish
> This youth should say 'twere well, and only therefore
> Desire to breed by me.

Yet her meaning does her honour. He must love her as he finds her. The theme of a lower class young woman – peasant, shepherdess, skivvy, even prostitute (there are countless variations) – capturing the heart of a young man of noble birth runs through English literature, and at all levels. It is an expression of that concern with "purity" – of blood, lineage, class – that so preoccupies and, certainly at a later time, disfigures social relations. The phrase "marrying beneath yourself" speaks volumes for the English obsession with class. This is not the place to enter into a discussion of why and how this obsession has taken such a grip on ways of thinking about social and personal relationships, but it is worth saying that *The Winter's Tale* gives abiding significance to the theme. We may think Shakespeare fudges the issue in that Perdita is of royal blood, so that an otherwise morganatic marriage to Florizel, let alone the possibility of miscegenation, is no more than glanced at. On the other hand, when Florizel binds himself to her, he does not know the truth about her parentage. In which case we have to consider whether it is nature or nurture that shows itself in what follows. For it is now that Perdita becomes so wonderful, so full of what 'nature' may be taken to mean.

*   *   *

There is, first of all, the giving of flowers, accomplished in poetry so purely beautiful that the temptation is simply to quote it all. But how witty Perdita is, too, and how delightful the wit. So, when Camillo, paying her a courtly compliment, says, "I should leave grazing, were I of your flock,/And only live by gazing", she replies:

> Out, alas!
> You'd be so lean that blasts of January
> Would blow you through and through.

And then, turning to Florizel and her young friends, she leads them to the front of the stage, lamenting the while her lack of spring flowers to give them:

> O Proserpina,
> For the flowers now that, frighted, thou let'st fall
> From Dis's wagon! Daffodils,
> That come before the swallow dares, and take
> The winds of March with beauty ...

"From Dis's wagon! Daffodils": the line lacks a metric foot. But if the actor speaking the line allows for a short break after "wagon" and then lingers on "Daffodils", the effect is wondrously to stitch sounds together (the *ds*, *as*, the repeated short *i*) so as to attune the auditors' ears to what will be the speech's shifting pace, its sensuous use of sound patterns, its sheer relish in a wide range of vocal, sonic possibilities. Anyone in any doubt as to this has only to speak the lines to understand how Shakespeare makes your mouth do lovely things, thrills your ear and, of course, the mind and emotions, too.

For Perdita's speech is about love, procreation, celebrated as in accord with nature because answering to Great Nature's laws. In an almost miraculous fashion her words blend together Christian and pagan: "Bright Phoebus in his strength," for example, is at once the resurgence of Glad Day, the newly arisen year, Apollo, the sun god who is also a ripener of wombs, and Christ, come to redeem the earth from its deathly winter. It is in this sense that what speaks through Perdita is Nature far more than Nurture. And although we may, if we so wish, claim that no un-nurtured shepherdess could have known of Proserpina, Juno, Cytherea or Phoebus, we have then to add that such Nurture does no more than vindicate Nature.

It is Nature that will out when Perdita longs for garlands for her women companions, and for "my sweet friend/To strew him o'er and o'er!"

Florizel: What, like a corse?

Perdita: No, like a bank for Love to lie and play on,
             Not like a corse; or if not to be buried,
             But quick and in mine arms.

And at that point she must suit the action to her words. Though her embrace is more than the formal hand-clasp of hospitality, it comes from one who is truly hospitable. This too is in accord with Nature, as Florizel's love for her testifies:

> ... when you do dance, I wish you
> A wave o' th' sea, that you might ever do
> Nothing but that ...

Perdita is the embodiment of Nature. But then, as Florizel draws Perdita to one side, ("But come, our dance, I pray/Your hand, my Perdita"), we are free to concentrate again on the disguised Polixenes and Camillo. Polixenes says, almost in wonderment:

> This is the prettiest low-born lass that ever
> Ran on the greensward: nothing she does or seems
> But smacks of something greater than herself,
> Too noble for this place.

> *Camillo*: He tells her something
> That makes her blood look out. Good sooth, she is
> The queen of curds and cream.

Camillo's compliment is generously intended but in identifying Perdita with country ways it can hardly reassure Polixenes.

*   *   *

Here a dance of Shepherds and Shepherdesses.
Whatever the dance is – and most editors assume it will have been some sort of Morris dance – it implies concord between the dancers, who include Florizel and Perdita. Polixenes asks the Shepherd for information about the young man who dances with his daughter, and the Shepherd tells him not merely that Florizel is of "worthy feeding", but that his avowed love for Perdita must be genuine: "for never gazed the moon/Upon the water as he'll stand and read,/As 'twere, my daughter's eyes". And finally, the Shepherd tells Polixenes that if "young Doricles/Do light upon her, she shall bring him that/Which he not dreams of." He means that her dowry will be the "fairy gold"

that Antigonus had left beside the infant Perdita. Although the phrase "worthy feeding" does not appear in Eric Partridge's *Dictionary of Slang and Unconventional English*, he does include as one meaning of "feeder", "a silver spoon", and Florizel was undoubtedly born with a silver spoon in his mouth, as the saying goes. Moreover, the use of "feed" to mean pasture lands is still current. It is then natural for the Shepherd to coin the phrase "worthy feeding", although only a gifted dramatist would have given it to him. But it took a great one to prompt the comparison between Florizel's intent gaze at Perdita and the moon upon the water. The moon is both separate from and yet absorbed into the water, its image contained within it, as Florizel is both apart from and drawn into Perdita's eyes, reflected in them. I have no doubt that this image must have been somewhere lodged in Keats' mind when he came to write his sonnet, 'Bright Star', which he notes was "Written on a Blank Page in Shakespeare's Poems, facing 'A Lover's Complaint'". But there is nothing opportunistic in Shakespeare giving this image to the Shepherd. It is further proof, if that were needed, that the Shepherd's care for Perdita is prompted by a disinterested, loving regard, and that his generosity of spirit speaks, if not volumes, then a natural eloquence.

Not that Polixenes is likely to be bothered by such consideration. But before he can speak again a servant enters with news that a pedlar is at the door, who can entertain with songs. The Clown bids the servant bring the pedlar in.

Enter Autolycus singing.
The song is one encouraging those present to buy from him. And buy they do, although the Clown complains that his pocket has been picked, allowing the man who picked it to commiserate with him: "And indeed, sir, there are cozeners abroad: therefore it behoves men to be wary." Autolycus' impudent wit is put to further use in his advertising of ballads for sale, including ones he says, that tell of the latest town news, as broadsheet ballads certainly did, although it is unlikely that many featured tales of "how a usurer's wife was brought to bed of twenty money-bags at a burden, and how she longed to eat adders' heads and toads carbonadoed," let alone the other, wildly funny ballads that Autolycus has with him – presumably pinned to a thin lathe or branch torn from a tree.

More singing, then the servant re-enters, this time to say that there are outside "three carters, three shepherds, three neat-herds, three swine-herds, that have made themselves all men of hair", that they call themselves "Saltiers" (which is no doubt intended as a comic corruption of "satyrs"), and that they have a dance which is a "gallimaufry of gambols."

* * *

The Shepherd isn't keen on this dance. There has been "too much homely foolery already. I know, sir, we weary you." Polixenes reassures him by saying that "You weary those that refresh us. Pray, let's see these four threes of herdsmen". But the mood is beginning to turn sour. The entries of first Autolycus and now the men dressed as satyrs taint the idyll associated with Perdita and the dance of shepherds and shepherdesses: exploitation and rank sexuality have invaded, and to an extent taken possession of, the country scene. (The coarsening of atmosphere puts me in mind of Beethoven's 6th Symphony, the 'Pastoral', where the dance measure of the third movement becomes increasingly wild and out of control until it breaks down under the mutterings of the oncoming storm, its harmonies shredded by violent discord.) And it would certainly seem appropriate for the music that accompanies the satyrs' dance to be different in kind from that which played for the dance of shepherds and shepherdesses, wilder, shadowed by turbulence.

As the dance finishes, and the satyrs presumably exit, we hear Polixenes speak: "O, father, you'll know more of that hereafter." Then, to Camillo, "Is it not too far gone? 'Tis time to part them./ He's simple and tells much." Assuming "he" refers to the Shepherd, most commentators agree that while the dance has been going on, Polixenes has been drawing the Shepherd out, so that telling him he'll "know more of that hereafter" may then be in reply to some question of the Shepherd's – such as "Who are you?" But this would suppose the Shepherd has become troubled by the two guests, or that their presence has made him apprehensive, which can hardly be the case, given that some 40 lines later he invites Florizel and Perdita to take hands in marriage, and says to the disguised Polixenes and Camillo:

And, friends unknown, you shall bear witness to't.
I give my daughter to him, and will make
Her portion equal his.

I suggest that in saying that "you'll know more of that hereafter",
Polixenes, whether intending the Shepherd by "father" or (and why
not?) speaking to himself, has been affected by the mood of the satyrs'
dance, is contemplating coming troubles, may even be recalling his
erstwhile friend's terrible fall into the madness of sexual jealousy,
and wants to prevent it from happening again. I also think that he
has been more troubled by Perdita's innocent beauty than he can
acknowledge, and although the evidence of this doesn't emerge until
a little later, it has already made its mark.

But for now he 'tests' Florizel by asking the youth why he
hasn't bought "knacks" for his love. Florizel replies that Perdita
"prizes not such trifles as these are." Then he turns to her:

> I take thy hand, this hand
> As soft as dove's down and as white as it,
> Or Ethiopian's tooth, or the fanned snow that's bolted
> By th' northern blasts twice o'er –

Polixenes: What follows this?
> How prettily the young swain seems to wash
> The hand was fair before!

Florizel's hyperbolic language here is conventional enough. (It also
recalls that famous moment in *Romeo and Juliet* where Romeo likens
Juliet to "a rich jewel in an Ethiope's ear"). The taking of hands is,
too, conventional. But here it is bound to seem to the two disguised
onlookers as dangerously transgressive. The gesture of amity, because
it signifies love between prince and peasant, contradicts the social
order, is *anti*-pastoral.

And so, when the Shepherd, intent on their marriage, bids them
again to take each other's hand, Polixenes intervenes: "Have you a
father?" And from now on, as Florizel with increased vehemence
rejects Polixenes' repeated requests that the young man tell his father
of his marriage plans, we in the audience know the storm is about to
break. When it does, it is with terrible brutality:

> Thou, old traitor,
> I am sorry that by hanging thee I can
> But shorten thy life one week – And thou, fresh
>   piece
> Of excellent witchcraft, who, of force must know
> The royal fool thou cop'st with –

Shepherd: O, my heart!

Polixenes: I'll have thy beauty scratched with briers and made
More homely than thy state.

He then orders Florizel to "follow us to the court", before turning back to the shepherd and Perdita. The former he will, he says, free from "the dread blow" of death. (An odd moment, and perhaps a textual corruption, because nobody appears to take any notice of it, and both Camillo and the Shepherd continue to believe that the latter is sentenced to die.) As for Perdita:

> ... you, enchantment,
> Worthy enough a herdsman – yea, him too,
> That makes himself, but for our honour therein,
> Unworthy thee – if ever henceforth thou
> These rural latches to his entrance open,
> Or hoop his body more with thy embraces,
> I will devise a death as cruel for thee
> As thou art tender to't.

To call Perdita a piece of witchcraft and an enchantment is sufficient to explain Polixenes' cast of mind. For these are words of severe condemnation. She has used black arts to catch Florizel. Yet Polixenes is not immune to these arts. Not only does he pay her the tortuous compliment of admitting her beauty would be worthy of Florizel were he not a prince (although one who has lowered himself to be unworthy of her), but he so fears the power of her beauty that he threatens her not once, but twice, and in a manner that is purely sadistic. Her beauty will be "scratched with briers", and he will "devise" an especially cruel death for her. Among the meanings of the verb "devise" are "to plan, contrive" and "to plot in an artful, underhand way". Polixenes' threat may be that of a tyrannical king, but it is also, I am certain, prompted by an anguished, frustrated sexuality. For that knotted compliment betrays Polixenes' very real sense of Perdita's innocent allure. And as Hermione's display of hospitality had inflamed Leontes' jealousy, so Perdita's candid display of affection – hooping Florizel's body with her embraces – disturbs Polixenes. Like Leontes he has to fall back on a display of power and authority in order to try to control what ultimately lies beyond his or any one else's control: that of great, creating Nature. And note that at first he is so disturbed by her beauty, that he even pays his respects by addressing her as *you* – "you enchantment" – before returning to the more to be expected "thou" and "thee". Shakespeare intends us to notice this slippage, wants us to know how Polixenes is momentarily mastered by his sense of Perdita's worth before he can master himself and her.

The king's outburst dispels for once and for all any dream that rural Bohemia can be imagined as the corrective vision to the tainted court of Leontes' Sicilia. Hence Perdita's awakening to reality. Though she knows the injustice of Polixenes' authority:

> I was about to speak and tell him plainly
> The selfsame sun that shines upon his court
> Hides not his visage from our cottage, but
> Looks on alike.

the fact is that in the king's presence she was cowed into silence. Now she faces the truth:

> Will't please you, sir, be gone?
> I told you what would come of this. Beseech you,
> Of your own state take care. This dream of mine –
> Being now awake, I'll queen it no inch farther,
> But milk my ewes, and weep.

There is a barb lurking in the word "state". Look after yourself, Perdita tells Florizel, but also, from now on remember you are a prince and therefore, I implore you, don't dangle "queenly" dreams before the eyes of other innocent girls.

Polixenes' terrible anger having fallen on the Shepherd, too, the old man grieves that now: "Some hangman must put on my shroud and lay me/Where no priest shovels in dust." Then even he turns on

Perdita, calling her a cursed wretch "That knewst this was the prince, and wouldst adventure/To mingle faith with him!" Hospitality, family concord, is now shattered. The power of kings is truly frightening. But Florizel refuses to be frightened. Perdita reminds him how often she had warned him that "my dignity would last/But till 'twere known", to which Florizel replies:

> It cannot fail but by
> The violation of my faith and then;
> Let Nature crush the sides o' th' earth together
> And mar the seeds within! Lift up thy looks.
> From my succession wipe me, father, I
> Am heir to my affection.

As he tells Perdita to lift up her looks he will surely take her gently under the chin. The gesture, the touch, brings them together again. And thus strengthened, Florizel swears his faithfulness to Perdita, vows that he will not break his oath: "To this my fair beloved."

At this point Camillo finds himself involved in helping the pair escape Bohemia, as he had years earlier helped Polixenes escape Sicilia. But now he plans a return to the place from which he fled, because he has had true report of Leontes' repentance, and:

> Methinks I see
> Leontes opening his free arms and weeping
> His welcomes forth ...

Camillo, that is, imagines Leontes displaying exactly the generous hospitality that had once been the cause of such trouble to Sicilia and has now brought fear to Bohemia. Besides, he adds:

> Prosperity's the very bond of love,
> Whose fresh complexion and whose heart together
> Affliction alters.

> *Perdita*:   One of these is true:
> I think affliction may subdue the cheek,
> But not take in the mind.

Camillo:	Yea? Say you so?
	There shall not at your father's house these seven years
	Be born another such.

Florizel:	My good Camillo,
	She is as forward of her breeding as
	She is i' th' rear 'our birth.

Camillo:	I cannot say 'tis pity
	She lacks instructions, for she seems a mistress
	To most that teach.

There is, surely, an extraordinary tenderness about Camillo's speaking to Perdita here. That "Yea? Say you so?" is amused, but at the same time wonderstruck. He too, note, addresses her as "you". And in what follows we return yet again to the issue of nature and nurture, to the inherent and the acquired. The mood of the scene at this point is recovering some of the sweetness that had characterised its middle portion. At which point:

Enter Autolycus.
In his poem, 'Autolycus', MacNeice remarks how in the last plays Shakespeare balances the wind that blows kindly on "Marinas, Perditas":

> With what we knew already, gabbing earth
> Hot from Eastcheap – Watch your pockets when
> That rogue comes round the corner, he can slit
> Purse-strings as quickly as his maker's pen
> Will try your heartstrings in the name of mirth.

Now, this piece of "gabbing earth" reveals that he is still up to his tricks. He has sold all his bits of trumpery, and in addition "picked and cut most of their festival purses". "Out of the bent timber of humanity nothing straight can be made", Kant famously said, by way of rebuking those idealists who thought it possible that human nature could be "born again". He might have had Autolycus in mind.

What happens next is perfect for this rogue. Camillo, Florizel and Perdita discover him and get him to exchange clothes with the young prince. Realising what they are up to, he says as they free him: "If I thought it were a piece of honesty to acquaint the King withal, I would not do't. I hold it the more knavery to conceal it; and therein am I constant to my profession." No sooner has he uttered the words than he gets the chance to be, as he says, honest by chance. For the Clown and Shepherd now enter and Autolycus overhears them deciding to tell Polixenes that Perdita is not the Shepherd's daughter but a changeling, who had with her fairy gold.

Autolycus has now the opportunity to use his wit to confuse, harry, and indeed torment the hapless father and son. His posturing as a courtier and swordsman, while very funny, at the same time raises questions about true breeding. When the Shepherd asks him, "Are you a courtier, an't like you, sir?" Autolycus answers:

> Whether it like me or no, I am a courtier. Seest thou not the air of the court in these enfoldings? Hath not my gait in it the measure of the court? Receives not thy nose court-odour from me? Reflect I not on thy baseness court-contempt? Think'st thou, for that I insinuate, to toaze from thee thy business, I am therefore no courtier? ...
> How blessed are we that are not simple men!
> Yet nature might have made me as these are:
> Therefore I'll not disdain.

As he speaks, Autolycus will be mincing about the stage, flirting his borrowed dress, breathing in the men's faces, perhaps bringing his armpit close to their noses, tilting his nose to the air and pursing his lips to show his court contempt of them. Such parody of superior manners is the comic revenge of those who are excluded from admission to the higher social echelons on the ones who exclude them, and you can find it in all societies and at all times: from the Aristophanic satire of ancient Greece to the 20th century cakewalk, invented by poor blacks in the deep south of the USA as a ribald imitation of white people's dance style.

"Yet Nature might have made me as these are." Has nature made Autolycus what he is? Well, yes, in that it has made him quick-witted. But nurture has made him adept at pursuing the main chance whenever it offers itself, as it does here. For he terrorises the pair into believing that, as he is a courtier and has influence over the king, they should hand him yet more money if he is to bring them to the royal presence. And he does this by pretending not to know who they are and so telling of the fate that lies in store for the Shepherd and his son, who shall:

> ... be flayed alive; then 'nointed over with honey, set on the head of a wasps' nest; then stand till he be three-quarters and a dram dead; then recovered again with aqua-vitae or some other hot infusion; then, raw as he is, and in the hottest day prognostication proclaims, shall he be set against a brick wall, the sun looking with a southward eye upon him, where he is to behold him with flies blown to death.

It isn't difficult to imagine the relish with which Autolycus will roll such phrases as "hot infusion" and "prognostication proclaims" round his tongue, nor how he will draw out his description of the tortures awaiting the Clown. It is grotesquely comic. It is also further evidence of a superabundance of inventive wit that we had witnessed in Autolycus' recommendation of ballads and that, as commentators note, is in the last analysis proof positive of Shakespeare's own endlessly fertile imagination, one that often bursts out in his comic characters. (It is this exuberant largesse which, I have no doubt, licensed Dickens' writing about such characters as Quilp and Mrs Gamp, comic grotesques whose language overflows with an Autolycus-like excess.)

But Autolycus' extravagant imaginings would also remind Shakespeare's audience of the whispers that went about of how torture was used at James' court and of how men bought into royal favour by an expressed willingness to do the king's business for him. And although I don't want to make heavy weather of this (we are not dealing with the murderers in *Macbeth*) we have just seen that lives can be forfeit to a king's whim and that his displeasure, however unreasonable or unjust, can bring with it a sentence of death.

5

Reconciliations

With the beginning of Act V we move from the tainted world of Bohemia to the cleansed world of Sicilia.

Enter Leontes, Cleomenes, Dion, Paulina, Servants: Florizel, Perdita. Thus the Folio, although as Florizel and Perdita are also given an entry later in the scene this must be an error. What matters is that those who do enter form, as it were, a *cordon sanitaire*. We last saw Cleomenes and Dion delivering the oracle's truth to Leontes, having journeyed with it back from where "The climate's delicate, the air most sweet". Now, Cleomenes, the first to speak, tells the penitent Leontes:

> Sir, you have done enough, and have performed
> A saint-like sorrow. No fault could you make
> Which you have not redeemed ...
> > At the last,
> Do as the heavens have done, forget your evil;
> With them forgive yourself.

But Leontes' awareness of what he has destroyed – "the sweet'st companion that e'er man/Bred his hopes out of" – will not allow him to forget "The wrong I did myself". He means both the wrong he did to himself as king, losing an heir, losing wife and children, and the wrong he himself did. That is, he takes full responsibility for his actions:

> I made this, I have forgotten
> And remember ...
> Made this unknowing, half conscious, unknown, my own.

With due allowance made for inevitable differences, these lines, uttered or at least articulated by the unnamed male consciousness of T.S. Eliot's 'Marina', might be speaking for Leontes. And Paulina, that voice of unremitting conscience, concurs with his acknowledgement of the wrong he has done:

> If one by one you wedded all the world,
> Or from the all that are took something good
> To make a perfect woman, she you killed
> Would be unparalleled.

> *Leontes*:   I think so. Killed!
> She I killed! I did so; but thou strik'st me
> Sorely to say I did. It is as bitter
> Upon thy tongue as in my thought. Now, good now,
> Say so but seldom.

Cleomenes backs up Leontes' appeal but Paulina will have none of it: "You are one of those/Would have him wed again."

Dion now joins in. Yes, he says, Leontes should wed again, for the sake of the state:

> What dangers by his highness' fail of issue
> May drop upon his kingdom and devour
> Incertain lookers-on.

By "lookers-on" Dion must mean those within the state who are unsure how to behave as citizens and who therefore need strong leadership to be kept in order. This is a political argument for the strong leader, and we should recall that in 1610/11 James had succeeded to a throne left vacant at the death of Elizabeth, the "virgin queen" who had failed of issue. I don't suspect Dion's remark of containing a hidden barb directed at James' rule, but it certainly touches on a subject close to the hearts of people living under an absolute monarch.

But again Paulina is unimpressed:

> ... the gods
> Will have fulfilled their secret purposes ...
>   'Tis your counsel

My lord should to the heavens be contrary,
Oppose against their wills. (*To Leontes*) Care not for issue.
The crown will find an heir. Great Alexander
Left his to th' worthiest; so his successor
Was like to be the best.

She speaks for piety, for acceptance of a grand design beyond human understanding. And though the apparent common sense of her claim that a fit successor to the throne can always be found will look suspect the moment we consider the evidence from history, it at least directs Leontes away from state considerations towards others she regards as far more important, above all, of course, the destruction of his marriage, of his wife and, for all anyone knows to the contrary, of both his children. And she gets her way. Leontes promises never to marry "Unless another,/As like Hermione as is her picture,/Affront his eye."

*　　*　　*

Enter a Servant.
The servant comes with news that Prince Florizel, son of Polixenes, and his princess "desires access/To your high presence." The gods' secret purposes are now moving to their conclusion. In Louis MacNeice's poem we are told that "In his last phase when hardly bothering/To be a dramatist, the Master turned away/From his taut plots and complex characters/To tapestried romances." But this is hardly fair to the plotting of *The Winter's Tale* (nor to characters who, if they lack the complexity of those to be found in the great tragedies, are nonetheless far more than two-dimensional figures on a brocade). The plotting at this juncture beautifully prepares for the play's last movement. For as the servant tells Leontes of the beauty of Florizel's princess, Paulina bursts out:

O Hermione,
As every present time doth boast itself
Above a better gone, so must thy grave
Give way to what's seen now.

She speaks with angry or despairing sarcasm. But she also, unknown to herself, speaks a deeper truth. For the young woman about to

59

appear is, in truth, Hermione's daughter, so that Hermione in her has risen from the grave. As for Florizel, Paulina remarks that:

> Had our prince
> Jewel of children, seen this hour, he had paired
> Well with this lord: there was not full a month
> Between their births.

Leontes: Prithee, no more! Cease! Thou know'st
> He dies to me again when talked of.

There may be a pitilessness about Paulina's truth telling, but she is not malicious. And in giving her such authority over the king, Shakespeare is manifestly choosing to oppose the conventional religious and social dictum that women should be subservient to and obedient to, men.

With the entry of Florizel and Perdita, Leontes takes on himself the role of hospitable welcomer. He also pays gracious compliment to the young man's parentage in a manner that inevitably recalls his own earlier self's frenzy of doubt:

> Your mother was most true to wedlock, Prince:
> For she did print your royal father off,
> Conceiving you ...
>   Most dearly welcome,
> And your fair princess – goddess! O Alas!
> I lost a couple that 'twixt heaven and earth
> Might thus have stood, begetting wonder, as
> You, gracious couple, do. And then I lost –
> All mine own folly – the society,
> Amity too, of your brave father ...

There is not much doubt that it is when Leontes brings himself to look at Perdita that he is prompted, almost without willing it, to confess his past. "Goddess", he calls her. This is well beyond conventional compliment. The word is uttered involuntarily. The Folio has the line as "And your fair princess (goddess) oh: alas". The punctuation sufficiently indicates the perturbation in Leontes' mind at the sight of Perdita. He must, surely, see in her some semblance of his lost wife, and this, then, reminds him of the children he also lost.

It is without doubt intensely moving, this meeting of father and daughter, neither of whom knows of their relationship, although it is her appearance that stirs the ageing man to a sweetness of expression that is new. 'Welcome hither,' he says to them again, "As is the spring to th' earth", and the resonance of that simile, its suggestion of regeneration, hardly needs to be pointed out.

Moreover, his welcome to them is accompanied by a blessing that is part of his new spirit:

> The blessèd gods
> Purge all infection from our air whilst you
> Do climate here!

This is a new Leontes, or perhaps it is better to say that this is a newly attentive Leontes, one whose consideration for others tells of a humanising that shines through in his repeated acknowledgement of his past sins:

> What might I have been,
> Might I a son and daughter now have looked on,
> Such goodly things as you!

There is an innocent irony here. Leontes is in fact looking at his daughter and son-in-law. But with the arrival of a lord a deeper irony breaks in on his words, for the lord comes to tell Leontes that Bohemia – that is, Polixenes:

> Desires you to attach his son, who has –
> His dignity and duty both cast off –
> Fled from his father, from his hopes, and with
> A shepherd's daughter.

The lord further tells Leontes that Camillo is with Polixenes and that they are accompanied by "The father of this seeming lady, and/ Her brother." That everyone should now be converging on Leontes' court may not be what MacNeice had in mind as "taut plotting", but it is pretty well carpentered in order to ensure that matters can now be brought to a conclusion. Only one more element needs to be fitted into place in this scene. In response to Florizel's admission that he and Perdita are not in fact married and that he wishes Leontes would act as their advocate for "at your request/My father will grant precious things as trifles", the king says:

> Would he do so, I'd beg your precious mistress,
> Which he counts but a trifle.

Paulina: Sir, my liege,
Your eye hath too much youth in't. Not a month
'Fore your queen died she was more worth such gazes
Than what you look on now.

Leontes: I thought of her
Even in these looks I made.

"Which he counts but a trifle" has to be spoken in a mixture of wondering disbelief and deep tenderness. How can anyone think of this woman as a "trifle", is the meaning. Hence, Paulina's rebuke. Hence, too, Leontes' reply to her, made, I suggest, without his taking his eyes off Perdita. It isn't that he sees his daughter, but that in Perdita he now sees his wife.

That is to say, in the figure of Perdita, Leontes registers the essence of Hermione. And with that alive in him, he goes to meet Polixenes.

*   *   *

The scene that follows may seem an anti-climax, at best a convenient way of speeding the narrative to its conclusion. For in it, Autolycus, who we assume is on his way to Leontes' court, learns that the Shepherd has managed to explain to Polixenes the circumstances of his discovery of Perdita and that as a result "The oracle is fulfilled: the King's daughter is found." And, as this discovery of Perdita's origins is announced, a third gentleman enters to say that Antigonus' letters have been discovered and that the proof positive that Perdita is Hermione's daughter lies in "the affection of nobleness which nature shows above her breeding". Once more the play's major terms come before us, and this time with confirmation that the one, nature, being inherent, is of far greater worth than nurture, which is extrinsic, acquired as are clothes and manners.

It may seem, though, that Shakespeare has missed a trick. Why not show us the "discovery" of Perdita? Why have it reported and so lose a dramatic opportunity? The answer, of course, is that he wants to save all for the final denouement, does not intend to weaken the impact of what will be the culminating *coup de théâtre,* the moment that will confirm that the play is, as one of the gentlemen here says, "like an old play still."

But for now we have the discomforting comeuppance of Autolycus by Shepherd and Clown, who play out a comic version of the debate about nature and nurture. Having been rewarded for their care of Perdita, they happen on their tormentor, and the Clown immediately challenges him to say:

> I am not now a gentleman born.

Autolycus: I know you are now, sir, a gentleman born.

Clown: Ay, and have been so any time these four hours.

Shepherd: And so have I, boy.

Clown: So you have; but I was a gentleman born before my father: for the King's son took me by the hand, and called me brother; and then the two kings called my father brother; and then the Prince my brother and the Princess my sister called my father father. And so we wept; and there was the first gentleman-like tears that ever we shed.

Comic, yes, but if the Clown comes across as little more than an amiable and credulous buffoon, the Shepherd is made of finer stuff, and although treated with a genial comic hand, he is also, as we have seen, someone of substantial worth. That father and son are brought within the newly-harmonious circle of the courts indicates the kind of reconciliation to which the masque aspires and to which Shakespeare's comedies all tend, though never so as to include all. Autolycus, we can be sure, will not mend his ways. And although Autolycus isn't as powerful, or as threatening, a presence as Malvolio or Caliban, his recalcitrance is real enough.

*   *   *

But in this play the threat Autolycus poses is easily contained. The real threat to harmony lies elsewhere, in the two kings who, in their different ways, endanger lives and social wellbeing. No longer, though. Leontes is repentant, Polixenes reconciled to his friend and his son. And so:

Enter Leontes, Polixenes, Florizel, Perdita, Camillo, Paulina; Hermione (like a statue:) lords, &c.

They are here to view the statue of Hermione that has been so long in the carving, Paulina tells them. Before it is unveiled Leontes pays deep, heartfelt tribute to "grave and good Paulina," and to "the great comfort/That I have had of thee." Grave and good. These virtues are different from the warrior-like anger of her earlier self. She, too, has changed with the passage of years. But then the image of Time as discoverer of truth cannot be dissevered from the fact that, as Sonnet 12 has it, "nothing 'gainst Time's scythe can make defence." And so, as Leontes, gazing at the statue, says:

> But yet, Paulina,
> Hermione was not so much wrinkled, nothing
> So agèd as this seems.

Polixenes: O, not by much!

Paulina: So much the more our carver's excellence,
> Which lets go by some sixteen years and makes her
> As she lived now.

Leontes: As now she might have done,
> So much to my good comfort as it is
> Now piercing to my soul.

Shakespeare's first audience would not have known the statue was about to come to life. There must always be people who are seeing the play for the first time and who will therefore not know what to make of what they witness. But what is unmissable is the quality of Leontes' response, for which even the word "piercing" seems too weak. There is an almost unbearable blend of anguish and yearning in the way he addresses what he calls this "royal piece", and the comfort he receives from Polixenes and the steadfast Camillo intensifies the wrought-up emotion. And so, eventually, Paulina tells him she can make the statue move, and that the art by which she will do this is not unlawful (isn't in other words black magic.) "Music, awake her, strike!" she orders, and then, to the statue, "'Tis time: descend."

As all commentators note, music is integral to the reviving of Hermione, functions, in Wilson Knight's words, as the "specifically releasing agent." Music also accompanies the awakening of Thais from her trance in *Pericles* (Act III, scene 2), as it accompanies the moment when Lear recovers from his madness. Indeed, the Doctor who attends Lear specifically requests "Louder the music there" and Cordelia says "Restoration hang/The medicine on my lips", as she kisses her father and so brings him back to life. There is no space here, nor is there the need, to go into detail about the long-held conviction that certain forms of music have curative and restorative powers, that their harmonies awaken lost or disturbed harmonies in the human frame, soul, consciousness, call it what you will. Enough to note that here as the music begins to play, so the statue of Hermione stirs, is transformed, and becomes a living person:

> *Leontes*:   O, she's warm!
> If this be magic, let it be an art
> Lawful as eating.

The king instinctively identifies Paulina's magic, and Hermione's return to life, as a function that is intrinsic to entertainment, hospitality. But how has this been managed?

> *Paulina*:   That she is living,
> Were it but told you, should be hooted at
> Like an old tale.

It is a moment of supreme daring. The master dramatist has a character tell us that we have to believe the evidence of our eyes, even though we know we are witnessing an illusion. The old tale has become capable of bearing truth. I have seen many productions of *The Winter's Tale*, including some real stinkers, but this moment never fails to thrill me, because it is the vindication of all true dramatic art. This is and is not Hermione, is and is not a boy pretending to be a woman who is pretending to be a statue who then comes to life.

And, in a final twist in the plotting of things, Hermione is now introduced to the daughter she had thought dead and who is now the perfect image of the younger Hermione.

> You gods, look down,
> And from your sacred vials pour your graces
> Upon my daughter's head!

Here, for the last time, we find the gods invoked as benevolent guides of human actions. "Gods" because the ostensible setting of the play is pre-Christian. But as the "grave and good" Paulina is the person who has guided Leontes towards true repentance and has accomplished the restoration of his apparently dead queen, it is inevitable that Hermione's words have a Christian resonance, though one that specifically rejects Pauline dogma. Nor should we forget that all the crucial events in the play are set in motion by human action, *not* by divine intervention.

With Hermione's words sounding in our ears, and with Leontes offering Paulina "an honourable husband" in Camillo, the play ends, the circle of reconciliation now complete.

*　　*　　*

Except, of course, that the actors immediately return to dance for the audience. This is hardly ever referred to in editions of *The Winter's Tale* or any of the plays, but Matt Simpson rightly draws attention to the importance of such a dance. As he says towards the end of his study of *The Tempest*, the dance, often a jig or reel, "acts as a safety-valve for the emotions the play has aroused." It is one among several reasons to praise the company resident at the new Globe Theatre that the actors always end performances with a dance. At the end of the early comedy, *Love's Labours Lost*, there is a song sung by the entire cast which celebrates both spring ("When daisies pied and violets blue") and winter ("When icicles hang by the wall"). At the song's conclusion Armado says, "The words of Mercury are harsh after the songs of Apollo." Some editors have suggested that this was added by a stage-manager or someone else as a comment. But the words make perfect sense. Not only that, they hint at a return to the real world from the make-believe world of poetry (of which

Apollo was god.) And Armada then adds, in words frequently not given in editions of the play, "You that way; we this way." These words, too, make perfect sense. Stepping out of his role, Armado says to the audience: you are free to leave now, we must go back to the tiring room. Whatever dance accompanies the two-part song or comes at its conclusion rounds off the performance, and Armado's final words release the audience from its spectatorial role. It can now go back to active life.

And yet if I were directing a full production of *The Winter's Tale* I would end with a dance that was more than merely reel or jig, though I might want it to mutate into one. To explain why, let me quote from that essay by D.J. Gordon, on Ben Jonson's *Hymenaei*, to which I have already referred:

> The union of marriage consummated in love typifies the harmonious ordering of man's nature and man's society that follows when reason is obeyed; this is perfection ... In both microcosm and macrocosm right order has been established by the Divine Reason, and perfection, right order, is achieved and maintained when the dispositions of reason, human and divine, are admitted and accepted. The circle is eternity, perfection, God ... The circle is also the girdle of Venus, marriage that is a bond of union through love.

By all means let a patterned dance, of whatever kind, that brings everyone into a circle, break up into a jig. But let the pattern be there for a while at least, to symbolise the "right order" which at the end of Shakespeare's great play has been finally and after so much pain established as an image of Divine Reason or, if we wish to avoid such an exalted term, of a social harmony acceptable to all, or nearly all.

Coda

The National Gallery of Scotland in Edinburgh includes several paintings by Titian among its holdings. All of them are great, and one in particular preoccupies me. Called 'The Three Ages of Man', it is a painting I go to stand in front of every time I visit the city, and although I know it as well as I know any painting, it never fails to move me, to delight and reassure. Before I explain its special power, I had better describe it. Picture left (the right as you look) two babies are asleep on the ground, while a small, podgy cupid, arm looped round a dead tree stump or a stump perhaps about to burst into new life, attempts to waken them. To their right, in the middle background, an old man with a long grey beard sits on a raised hillock, contemplating two skulls which he holds in either hand. On the other side of the painting, filling more of the canvas, two lovers gaze into each other's eyes. The man, semi-naked, has a drowsy expression, the young woman's gaze is unwavering, intent, absorbed beyond any self-consciousness. If I had to choose one word to describe her look it would be 'ardent', but in truth no word or combination of words can do justice to the intentness of her 'speaking look'. Over and behind them is an abundance of greenery.

In 2002 the painting was lent to the National Gallery in London, for its big Titian exhibition. The catalogue entry for 'The Ages of Man' has this to say of the couple:

> The lovers gaze languidly into each other's eyes, although we know from X-rays that the girl had, at one time, been angled towards the spectator. [They] have just finished making music, and the suggestive position of one pipe, protruding from the youth's groin, implies that they have also been making love. This sensuality is clothed in Renaissance conventions: notably the male's amorous engagement is

indicated by his crossed legs and her overlapping arms, positions that were 'read' as the intertwining of lovers ... The girl's myrtle wreath, forever green, was symbolic of everlasting love, and in particular, of conjugal fidelity. The juxtaposition of a female more fully dressed than the male goes against Venetian pastoral convention. Perhaps in depicting the girl *dishabille* rather than nude Titian has rendered the image more provocative, her white shift, an undergarment not usually exposed, suggests an intimate narrative involving the process of undressing. She sensuously caresses his leg with the bare flesh of her arm.

Reading this I reflect that this is what happens when art history is divorced from an ability actually to *look* and *see*. (And if the couple have just been making love wouldn't the pipe "protruding from the youth's groin" be lying down rather than poking up?). But the unsaveable daftness of this account is most telling in the cataloguer's insistence that the two gaze "languidly" into each other's eyes· No. No. No. The young man, it's true, looks at the woman with a kind of sleepy intensity that suggests not desire fulfilled but expectant, but her look has absolutely nothing to do with languor. Though as I say, no words can be adequate to her gaze, perhaps the nearest to do it justice would be the Shepherd's report to Polixenes about how his son looks at Perdita: "Never gazed the moon/Upon the water as he'll stand and read,/As 'twere, my daughter's eyes."

This is why I draw attention to Titian's great painting. In its depiction of the young lovers I see Perdita and Florizel. More than that; in its inclusion of the young and old is embodied much of the meaning of *The Winter's Tale*. As the cataloguer, for once on safe ground, says, by showing the old man, who is surely Father Time, holding the two skulls – which we can imagine to be the lovers now gone to death as the babies had been their much younger selves – "the painting assumes the status of *memento mori*, whilst illustrating the promise of regeneration not only through renewal of human life but also spiritually, suggested by the church in the background." There is indeed a church, to picture right of and behind the figure of Father Time, although its presence is not more emphasised than are the gods in Shakespeare's play. Titian's commission, the cataloguer concludes "seems inspired by the genre of pastoral romance, evoking a mood rather than a specific text." Certainly a painting that was completed in 1511/12 cannot be inspired by a play written some hundred years later, any more than Shakespeare can have known Titian's work. It is congruence of imaginative intent we are talking about.

Yet even this may seem over-emphatic. For the obvious fact is that a painting exists in a world of space whereas a work of literature lives in a world of time. In a painting we can start where we like and finish where we like. Our eyes, no matter how skilfully the painter wants to conduct us through his painting, can in this instance range from lovers to babies to old man, back and forward, in any direction we choose. From birth to death to love to death to birth ... any sequence is possible. And indeed in this particular painting Titian makes no attempt to control how we 'read' the painting, how we should move from one point to another. We can start with Father Time or with the babies being prodded into wakefulness by Cupid. Or we can start with the lovers. My own hunch is that any spectator will start with them and that however the eye wanders to other points of the canvas, it is to the lovers that we will return.

I cannot, however, be certain that this will be so for all those who stand in front of the painting. But those who go to see a performance of *The Winter's Tale* have no alternative but to start at the beginning and to end where Shakespeare closes the play off. And even if in the solitude of a study a reader should choose to flick backwards and forwards, the plain fact is that the play needs to be read from Act I onwards. Yet the miracle of *The Winter's Tale* is that beginnings and endings are provisional, are not closed off, are, in fact, inclusive of each other. At the play's outset there are births and deaths; at the end there are marriages and renewals, but thoughts, also, of ageing and death. Yes, we live in a world of time, where Hermione's wrinkles are a truth to be acknowledged, and acts have consequences that cannot be wished away. But if time fares forward, from birth to death, time is also cyclic, bringing round new births and, who knows, new breakings of love. For who can be sure that at some future moment Florizel won't echo or at least remind grieving onlookers of his father or father in-law's mad cruelties? Who can predict that goodness won't be put upon, threatened and even overwhelmed by forces we would struggle not to call evil? All that we know of the world tells us that this is only too likely. And against such forces, how can beauty and goodness compete, whose action is no stronger than a flower? To say this brings me to one last point. In a late poem, 'To Bronislaw Z' the great 19th century Irish poet Cyprian Kamil Norwid (1821-1883) imagines his friend Bronislaw Zaleski asking him what he is writing. He replies:

> Well, I'm writing you this letter –
> But don't say I've sent you a token gift – *it's only poetry!*
> Poetry without gold is poor – but gold without her,
> I tell you, verily is *vanity of vanities* ...
> Varieties of opulence will crawl away and vanish,
> Treasures and powers blow away, whole communities shake,
> Of the things of this world only two will remain,
> Two only: *poetry and goodness* ... and nothing else ...
> Without them every skill will prove paper-thin,
> So weighty is the duality of these two! ...

> (C.K. Norwid, *Selected Poems*, trans. Adam Czerniawski,
> Anvil, 2004)

Even if we acknowledge that by "poetry" here, Norwid means more than verse-making, that he means the articulating of deep truths to be found in all the great arts, even then we may say that his belief in the durability of poetry and goodness itself seems paper thin. Given the horrors that the 20th century instigated and witnessed, could any sane person believe that poetry and goodness will alone remain?

Well, yes, is the answer. And not because hypocrisy is the tribute vice pays to virtue, so that even the blackest-hearted villain claims to be susceptible to both about because goodness has a vitality that is, literally, unkillable. We are often told that evil is more interesting than goodness, at all events in literature. This rests on the assumption – a very silly one – that goodness is passive, is acted upon, whereas evil is an actor. But Shakespeare, like all great artists, convincingly shows us goodness as an active principle. In *The Winter's Tale* it is Hermione who is first active, the embodiment of generous hospitality. When she is forced into passivity by being imprisoned, Paulina takes over as active agent of good. And in the second half of the play it is Perdita who becomes the intent embodiment of goodness, her inherent virtue as undeflectable as the gaze of the young woman in Titian's painting.

And this being so, it cannot be coincidence that the three woman have between them the play's great poetry. They *are* the poetry, whether this is in Hermione's playful speeches to Polixenes, the calm grandeur of what she says at her trial, or in Paulina's scalding denunciation of Leontes and her championing of his queen, or in the candid incorruptible sweetness of Perdita's flower speech or the truth-telling simplicity of "The selfsame sun that shines upon his court/ Hides not his visage from our cottage, but/Looks on alike." That after all *is* a truth, though the mighty and powerful may wish to deny it and do all they can to prevent its realisation.

Bibliography

Editions of *The Winter's Tale* consulted for this study:
As well as the Penguin text, edited by Ernest Schanzer, I have made use of the Arden edition, by J.H.P. Pafford, published by Methuen, because it has more detailed notes than those supplied by Schanzer. I have also referred to the Folio edition, published in facsimile by Paul Hamlyn, which no self-respecting library should be without.

General Studies of Shakespeare I have drawn on include, in alphabetical order:

Jonathan Bate, *The Genius of Shakespeare*, Picador, 1997.

Samuel Johnson, *Preface to Shakespeare*. This was originally published in 1765, as the introduction to Johnson's edition of the plays. It is readily available in modern editions of Johnson's works.

John Middleton Murry, *Shakespeare* (Jonathan Cape, 1936). Although difficult to come by, this is well worth hunting down, and Murry's discussion of *The Winter's Tale* is, for all its brevity, invaluable.

Anne Richter, *Shakespeare and the Idea of the Play* (Penguin, 1967). (Though in the first edition, the author's name is given as Anne Barton.)

John Wain, *The Living World of Shakespeare* (Penguin, 1964 and often reprinted). A first-rate general study which has much of value to say about the social life and dramatic conventions of Shakespeare's time.

I should add that Stephen Greenblatt's recent study of Shakespeare has been warmly recommended.

For especially useful studies of the play itself I recommend:

S.L. Bethell, *The Winter's Tale: A Study* (London, 1947). Bethell writes as a Catholic apologist, but this does not especially distort his account of the play and often, indeed, leads to important insights.

G. Wilson Knight, 'Great Creating Nature', in *The Crown of Life: Essays in Interpretation of Shakespeare's Final Plays* (Methuen, London, 1947). Good on symbolism and thematic metaphors, and as the book was written before Knight's loopy spiritualism took hold, it is to be recommended for its general good sense.

Bill Overton, *The Winter's Tale: The Critics Debate* (Macmillan, London, 1989). A shrewd, wide-ranging and admirable balanced review of the major (and some minor) critical approaches.

Other works consulted for or referred to in this study:

D.J. Gordon, *The Renaissance Imagination* (California University Press, Berkeley/London, 1975). Gordon's work on Masque is unlikely to be superseded, and tells you all you need to know about the form's importance for the Jacobean theatre.

Susanne K. Langer, *Feeling Into Form: a Theory of Art* (Routledge & Kegan Paul, London, 1953). Though in some ways close to Northrop Frye's famous and still influential *Anatomy of Criticism*, which appeared at about the same time and which, like Langer's work, considers genres and types, such as tragedy and comedy, in terms of overall structure and meaning, I prefer Langer as a more lucid guide.

Robert W. Malcolmson, *Popular Recreations in English Society 1700-1850* (Cambridge University Press, 1973). Malcolmson's work throws interesting and reliable light back on earlier customs, especially sheepshearing ceremonies and is thus of very real relevance to any attempt to understand what may be the meaning of the second half of Shakespeare's play.

Erwin Panofsky, *Studies in Iconology: Humanistic Themes in the Art of the Renaissance*, originally published by Oxford University Press, 1939, then, with additions and some emendations, by Harper, Torchback, in USA, 1962. You can learn more from Panofsky about the preoccupations of writers as well as artists in Renaissance Europe than from any number of literary historical works. His essay on 'Father Time', is not only a masterpiece in itself, but illuminates much in *The Winter's Tale*.

The poems by Louis MacNeice and William Carlos Williams discussed in the course of my monograph can be found in any good selections of their work.

GREENWICH EXCHANGE BOOKS

STUDENT GUIDES

Greenwich Exchange Student Guides are critical studies of major or contemporary serious writers in English and selected European languages. The series is for the student, the teacher and 'common readers' and is an ideal resource for libraries. The *Times Educational Supplement* praised these books, saying, "The style of these guides has a pressure of meaning behind it. Students should learn from that ... If art is about selection, perception and taste, then this is it."

(ISBN prefix 1-871551- applies)

All books are paperbacks unless otherwise stated

The series includes:

W.H. Auden by Stephen Wade (36-6)
Honoré de Balzac by Wendy Mercer (48-X)
William Blake by Peter Davies (27-7)
The Brontës by Peter Davies (24-2)
Robert Browning by John Lucas (59-5)
Samuel Taylor Coleridge by Andrew Keanie (64-1)
Joseph Conrad by Martin Seymour-Smith (18-8)
William Cowper by Michael Thorn (25-0)
Charles Dickens by Robert Giddings (26-9)
Emily Dickinson by Marnie Pomeroy (68-4)
John Donne by Sean Haldane (23-4)
Ford Madox Ford by Anthony Fowles (63-3)
The Stagecraft of Brian Friel by David Grant (74-9)
Robert Frost by Warren Hope (70-6)
Thomas Hardy by Sean Haldane (33-1)
Seamus Heaney by Warren Hope (37-4)
Gerard Manley Hopkins by Sean Sheehan (77-3)
James Joyce by Michael Murphy (73-0)
Philip Larkin by Warren Hope (35-8)
Poets of the First World War by John Greening (79-X)
Laughter in the Dark – The Plays of Joe Orton by Arthur Burke (56-0)
Philip Roth by Paul McDonald (72-2)
Shakespeare's *Macbeth* by Matt Simpson (69-2)
Shakespeare's *Othello* by Matt Simpson (71-4)
Shakespeare's *The Tempest* by Matt Simpson (75-7)
Shakespeare's Non-Dramatic Poetry by Martin Seymour-Smith (22-6)

Shakespeare's Sonnets by Martin Seymour-Smith (38-2)
Shakespeare's *The Winter's Tale* by John Lucas (80-3)
Tobias Smollett by Robert Giddings (21-8)
Dylan Thomas by Peter Davies (78-1)
Alfred, Lord Tennyson by Michael Thorn (20-X)
William Wordsworth by Andrew Keanie (57-9)

OTHER GREENWICH EXCHANGE BOOKS

LITERATURE & BIOGRAPHY

Matthew Arnold and 'Thyrsis' *by Patrick Carill Connolly*
Matthew Arnold (1822-1888) was a leading poet, intellect and aesthete of
the Victorian epoch. He is now best known for his strictures as a literary
and cultural critic, and educationist. After a long period of neglect, his
views have come in for a re-evaluation. Arnold's poetry remains less well
known, yet his poems and his understanding of poetry, which defied the
conventions of his time, were central to his achievement.
The author traces Arnold's intellectual and poetic development, showing
how his poetry gathers its meanings from a lifetime's study of European
literature and philosophy. Connolly's unique exegesis of 'Thyrsis' draws
upon a wide-ranging analysis of the pastoral and its associated myths in
both classical and native cultures. This study shows lucidly and in detail
how Arnold encouraged the intense reflection of the mind on the subject
placed before it, believing in " ... the all importance of the choice of the
subject, the necessity of accurate observation; and subordinate character
of expression."
Patrick Carill Connolly gained his English degree at Reading University
and taught English literature abroad for a number of years before returning
to Britain. He is now a civil servant living in London.
2004 • 180 pages • ISBN 1-871551-01-61-7

The Author, the Book and the Reader *by Robert Giddings*
This collection of essays analyses the effects of changing technology and
the attendant commercial pressures on literary styles and subject matter.
Authors covered include Charles Dickens, Tobias George Smollett, Mark
Twain, Dr Johnson and John le Carré.
1991 • 220 pages • illustrated • ISBN 1-871551-01-3

Aleister Crowley and the Cult of Pan *by Paul Newman*
Few more nightmarish figures stalk English literature than Aleister Crowley
(1875-1947), poet, magician, mountaineer and agent provocateur. In this

groundbreaking study, Paul Newman dives into the occult mire of Crowley's works and fishes out gems and grotesqueries that are by turns ethereal, sublime, pornographic and horrifying. Like Oscar Wilde before him, Crowley stood in "symbolic relationship to his age" and to contemporaries like Rupert Brooke, G.K. Chesterton and the Portuguese modernist, Fernando Pessoa. An influential exponent of the cult of the Great God Pan, his essentially 'pagan' outlook was shared by major European writers as well as English novelists like E.M. Forster, D.H. Lawrence and Arthur Machen.

Paul Newman lives in Cornwall. Editor of the literary magazine *Abraxas*, he has written over ten books.

2004 • 223 pages • ISBN 1-871551-66-8

John Dryden *by Anthony Fowles*

Of all the poets of the Augustan age, John Dryden was the most worldly. Anthony Fowles traces Dryden's evolution from 'wordsmith' to major poet. This critical study shows a poet of vigour and technical panache whose art was forged in the heat and battle of a turbulent polemical and pamphleteering age. Although Dryden's status as a literary critic has long been established, Fowles draws attention to Dryden's neglected achievements as a translator of poetry. He deals also with the less well-known aspects of Dryden's work – his plays and occasional pieces.

Born in London and educated at the Universities of Oxford and Southern California, Anthony Fowles began his career in film-making before becoming an author of film and television scripts and more than twenty books. Readers will welcome the many contemporary references to novels and film with which Fowles illuminates the life and work of this decisively influential English poetic voice.

2003 • 292 pages • ISBN 1-871551-58-7

The Good That We Do *by John Lucas*

John Lucas's book blends fiction, biography and social history in order to tell the story of his grandfather, Horace Kelly. Headteacher of a succession of elementary schools in impoverished areas of London, 'Hod' Kelly was also a keen cricketer, a devotee of the music hall, and included among his friends the great Trade Union leader Ernest Bevin. In telling the story of his life, Lucas has provided a fascinating range of insights into the lives of ordinary Londoners from the First World War until the outbreak of the Second World War. Threaded throughout is an account of such people's hunger for education, and of the different ways government, church and educational officialdom ministered to that hunger. *The Good That We Do* is both a study of one man and of a period when England changed, drastically and forever.

John Lucas is Professor Emeritus of the Universities of Loughborough and Nottingham Trent. He is the author of numerous works of a critical and scholarly nature and has published seven collections of poetry.

2001 • 214 pages • ISBN 1-871551-54-4

In Pursuit of Lewis Carroll *by Raphael Shaberman*

Sherlock Holmes and the author uncover new evidence in their investigations into the mysterious life and writing of Lewis Carroll. They examine published works by Carroll that have been overlooked by previous commentators. A newly discovered poem, almost certainly by Carroll, is published here.

Amongst many aspects of Carroll's highly complex personality, this book explores his relationship with his parents, numerous child friends, and the formidable Mrs Liddell, mother of the immortal Alice. Raphael Shaberman was a founder member of the Lewis Carroll Society and a teacher of autistic children.

1994 • 118 pages • illustrated • ISBN 1-871551-13-7

Liar! Liar!: Jack Kerouac – Novelist *by R.J. Ellis*

The fullest study of Jack Kerouac's fiction to date. It is the first book to devote an individual chapter to every one of his novels. *On the Road*, *Visions of Cody* and *The Subterraneans* are reread in-depth, in a new and exciting way. *Visions of Gerard* and *Doctor Sax* are also strikingly reinterpreted, as are other daringly innovative writings, like 'The Railroad Earth' and his "try at a spontaneous *Finnegans Wake*" – *Old Angel Midnight*. Neglected writings, such as *Tristessa* and *Big Sur*, are also analysed, alongside better-known novels such as *Dharma Bums* and *Desolation Angels*.

R.J. Ellis is Senior Lecturer in English at Nottingham Trent University.

1999 • 295 pages • ISBN 1-871551-53-6

Musical Offering *by Yolanthe Leigh*

In a series of vivid sketches, anecdotes and reflections, Yolanthe Leigh tells the story of her growing up in the Poland of the 1930s and the Second World War. These are poignant episodes of a child's first encounters with both the enchantments and the cruelties of the world; and from a later time, stark memories of the brutality of the Nazi invasion, and the hardships of student life in Warsaw under the Occupation. But most of all this is a record of inward development; passages of remarkable intensity and simplicity describe the girl's response to religion, to music, and to her discovery of philosophy.

Yolanthe Leigh was formerly a Lecturer in Philosophy at Reading University.
2000 • 57 pages • ISBN: 1-871551-46-3

Norman Cameron *by Warren Hope*
Norman Cameron's poetry was admired by W.H. Auden, celebrated by Dylan Thomas and valued by Robert Graves. He was described by Martin Seymour-Smith as, "one of ... the most rewarding and pure poets of his generation ..." and is at last given a full length biography. This eminently sociable man, who had periods of darkness and despair, wrote little poetry by comparison with others of his time, but it is always of a consistently high quality – imaginative and profound.
2000 • 221 pages • illustrated • ISBN 1-871551-05-6

POETRY

Adam's Thoughts in Winter *by Warren Hope*
Warren Hope's poems have appeared from time to time in a number of literary periodicals, pamphlets and anthologies on both sides of the Atlantic. They appeal to lovers of poetry everywhere. His poems are brief, clear, frequently lyrical, characterised by wit, but often distinguished by tenderness. The poems gathered in this first book-length collection counter the brutalising ethos of contemporary life, speaking of and for the virtues of modesty, honesty and gentleness in an individual, memorable way.
2000 • 47 pages • ISBN 1-871551-40-4

Baudelaire: Les Fleurs du Mal *Translated by F.W. Leakey*
Selected poems from *Les Fleurs du Mal* are translated with parallel French texts and are designed to be read with pleasure by readers who have no French as well as those who are practised in the French language.
F.W. Leakey was Professor of French in the University of London. As a scholar, critic and teacher he specialised in the work of Baudelaire for 50 years and published a number of books on the poet.
2001 • 153 pages • ISBN 1-871551-10-2

'The Last Blackbird' and other poems by Ralph Hodgson *edited and introduced by John Harding*
Ralph Hodgson (1871-1962) was a poet and illustrator whose most influential and enduring work appeared to great acclaim just prior to and during the First World War. His work is imbued with a spiritual passion for the beauty of creation and the mystery of existence. This new selection brings together, for the first time in 40 years, some of the most beautiful

and powerful 'hymns to life' in the English language.

John Harding lives in London. He is a freelance writer and teacher and is Ralph Hodgson's biographer.

2004 • 70 pages • ISBN 1-871551-81-1

Lines from the Stone Age *by Sean Haldane*

Reviewing Sean Haldane's 1992 volume *Desire in Belfast*, Robert Nye wrote in *The Times* that "Haldane can be sure of his place among the English poets." This place is not yet a conspicuous one, mainly because his early volumes appeared in Canada, and because he has earned his living by other means than literature. Despite this, his poems have always had their circle of readers. The 60 previously unpublished poems of *Lines from the Stone Age* – "lines of longing, terror, pride, lust and pain" – may widen this circle.

2000 • 53 pages • ISBN 1-871551-39-0

Shakespeare's Sonnets *by Martin Seymour-Smith*

Martin Seymour-Smith's outstanding achievement lies in the field of literary biography and criticism. In 1963 he produced his comprehensive edition, in the old spelling, of *Shakespeare's Sonnets* (here revised and corrected by himself and Peter Davies in 1998). With its landmark introduction and its brilliant critical commentary on each sonnet, it was praised by William Empson and John Dover Wilson. Stephen Spender said of him "I greatly admire Martin Seymour-Smith for the independence of his views and the great interest of his mind"; and both Robert Graves and Anthony Burgess described him as the leading critic of his time. His exegesis of the *Sonnets* remains unsurpassed.

2001 • 194 pages • ISBN 1-871551-38-2

The Rain and the Glass *by Robert Nye*

When Robert Nye's first poems were published, G.S. Fraser declared in the *Times Literary Supplement*: "Here is a proper poet, though it is hard to see how the larger literary public (greedy for flattery of their own concerns) could be brought to recognize that. But other proper poets – how many of them are left? – will recognize one of themselves."

Since then Nye has become known to a large public for his novels, especially *Falstaff* (1976), winner of the Hawthornden Prize and The Guardian Fiction Prize, and *The Late Mr Shakespeare* (1998). But his true vocation has always been poetry, and it is as a poet that he is best known to his fellow poets. "Nye is the inheritor of a poetic tradition that runs from Donne and Ralegh to Edward Thomas and Robert Graves," wrote James Aitchison in 1990, while the critic Gabriel Josipovici has described him as "one of the most interesting poets writing today, with a voice unlike that of any of his contemporaries".

This book contains all the poems Nye has written since his *Collected Poems* of 1995, together with his own selection from that volume. An introduction, telling the story of his poetic beginnings, affirms Nye's unfashionable belief in inspiration, as well as defining that quality of unforced truth which distinguishes the best of his work: "I have spent my life trying to write poems, but the poems gathered here came mostly when I was not."

2005 • 133 pages • ISBN 1-871551-41-2

Wilderness *by Martin Seymour-Smith*

This is Martin Seymour-Smith's first publication of his poetry for more than twenty years. This collection of 36 poems is a fearless account of an inner life of love, frustration, guilt, laughter and the celebration of others. He is best known to the general public as the author of the controversial and bestselling *Hardy* (1994).

1994 • 52 pages • ISBN 1-871551-08-0

BUSINESS

English Language Skills *by Vera Hughes*

If you want to be sure, (as a student, or in your business or personal life), that your written English is correct, this book is for you. Vera Hughes's aim is to help you to remember the basic rules of spelling, grammar and punctuation. 'Noun', 'verb', 'subject', 'object' and 'adjective' are the only technical terms used. The book teaches the clear, accurate English required by the business and office world. It coaches acceptable current usage and makes the rules easier to remember.

Vera Hughes was a civil servant and is a trainer and author of training manuals.

2002 • 142 pages • ISBN 1-871551-60-9